S0-AXQ-699

What you seed...
is what you get!

seeding your way to success...

Paul E. Tsika

Plow On Publications

Plow On Publications
a division of Paul E. Tsika Ministries, Inc.
Restoration Ranch
5351 Hwy. 71
Midfield, TX   77458

www.plowon.org

Printed in the United States of America

This book is dedicated to my grandchildren.

Psalm 128 *"All you who fear Yahweh, how blessed you are! How happily you walk on his smooth straight road! You worked hard and deserve all you've got coming. Enjoy the blessing! Revel in the goodness! Your wife will bear children as a vine bears grapes, your household lush as a vineyard, The children around your table as fresh and promising as young olive shoots. Stand in awe of God's Yes. Oh, how he blesses the one who fears Yahweh! Enjoy the good life in Jerusalem every day of your life. And enjoy your grandchildren. Peace to Israel!!"*

Proverbs 17:6 *"Children's Children are the crown of old men; and the glory of children are their fathers."*

As Billie and I look around our table, our hearts are filled with thanksgiving to our Lord for such a blessed family. Our cup runneth over, with our children and their spouses: Gretchen and Mark, Paul and Melanie, and Thom and Kelley plus 10 wonderful grandchildren. Our children are the heritage of the Lord and our grandchildren are the bumper crop of this family.

Meagan-18: "Our first, with a heart for Christ and a love for people and a desire to change the world."

Emily-16: "With great strength of heart and a passion to make a difference with her life."

Demetri-14: "A young man destined to be a leader among men."

Marissa-12: "Her carefree ways are contagious, her style is unique."

*Marlee-12: "Strong and determined, she will stand for what she believes."

*Shelby-11: "Just like her dad (Thom), witty, but passionate for what is right."

Zeke-11: "With a tender, but strong heart, he is a blessing to all who meet him."

Malory-10: "A special child... full of questions, suggestions and the joy of the Lord."

Jake-7: "Loves to please those he loves, funny and gifted with a great heart."

Kadie-2: "The caboose and crowning jewel of my heart. Who knows, but God, she'll be awesome."

*Will surely end up best friends—they are sooooo much alike.

ACKNOWLEDGEMENTS

I am continually thankful for those whom God has put in my life to empower me.

Therefore, I want to acknowledge:

Billie Kaye (my wife): who lights up my life and is truly the wind beneath my wings.

My Staff: Paul, Melanie, Thom and Kelley, who lighten my load everyday and set me free to do what I do.

Cynthia Mackey: for working together with me in designing the cover and organizing the layout. Thank you Cynthia.

Andrea Blaho: for editing, correcting, and helping you to read this book.

Wade Trimmer (my pastor): he has been my co-laborer in this project. He is a selfless man of God whose only concern is God being glorified and people being helped.

What You Seed is What You Get!

TABLE OF CONTENTS

What You Seed is What You Get!

FOREWORD BY WADE TRIMMER

As Paul and Billie Tsika's pastor, co-laborer in ministry, and friend for many years, I am highly honored to be afforded the opportunity of commending this book and its author to you. The book you hold in your hand is filled with good seeds. Read it carefully, begin sowing its principles consistently and patiently into your life and the lives of others and you will begin to "Seed" your way to a fruitful and successful harvest.

The principles that Paul enunciates in this book have been proven in his own life (both good "seeding" and bad "seeding," I might add). Among the numerous principles set forth, none has been more clearly and consistently practiced by Paul and Billie as the one stated as: "Taking the Risk of Investing in the Lives of Others Through Generous Distribution" (Cast your bread upon the waters, for you will find it after many days). Personally, I have never known people as generous and giving as are Paul and Billie! They have spent the last 35 years of their lives taking the risk of "seeding" or investing in the lives of others. They have generously and continuously sown the seeds of truth and wisdom of words in sermons, songs and speeches; in gifts of money and other material things; and above all else, tons of seeds of their precious time-involvement in loving friendships across this country.

1

What You Seed is What You Get!

Paul is one of the most encouraging examples of the harvest that comes from employing the principle of maintaining a Living-Giving Lifestyle. This lifestyle has brought in a harvest in which God has met their needs, multiplied their seed, and ministered to thousands through their deeds!

The truths set forth in this book will take you beyond just having a clear and compelling vision. Following its principles will empower you to understand that you must not only "see" yourself as being successful in your assignments, but that you must "seed" your dreams and visions with the things that carry the pattern for bringing what you see to fruition.

For example, if you "see" yourself in health, then you must "seed" yourself according to the things that make for healthy living. You can see yourself as slim and trim, fit and firm in muscle tone, but if you do not "seed" this vision with right and healthy eating habits, plenty of exercise and rest, along with a good, positive mental attitude, then you will reap only what you sowed and not what you saw!

If you "see" yourself with lots of friends, then you must "seed" yourself with a friendly attitude and approach to people.

If you "see" yourself as prosperous financially, then you must "seed" yourself in the principles of biblical giving and investment.

If you "see" your business expanding and enriching you and those under you, then you must "seed" yourself with the principles and practices that will reproduce your goals and dreams. Remember- What You SEED is What You Get!

The first step toward a great harvest is the step you make today. Make it forward, godly, well-aimed, and purposeful. Take the best seed with the right purpose, and start sowing it in the soil that will produce the harvest that God has designed for you. Remember, the steps you take today become the well-worn path of tomorrow.

My wife, Anne, and I wish to go on record in affirming our love, respect and appreciation for the loyal and loving friendship shown us by Paul and Billie. No one has befriended us, blessed us and borne with us for so long in so many loving and generous ways as have Paul and Billie! We love you and pray that the good seed that this book contains will be sown far and wide with a harvest that will go on paying dividends forever!

Pastor Wade and Anne Trimmer

Grace Fellowship Church, Augusta, Georgia

What You Seed is What You Get!

Chapter One:
Seed Your Dreams

One of the most important truths that I have ever embraced is the principle of seeding. In this book, I hope to explain why seeing means little unless you are willing to seed for your future. A successful life is determined not only by where you "see" yourself going, but by what you "seed" on a daily basis.

A successful life-farmer begins with "seeing" himself as being successful. People were designed with vision or foresight. Every person's success is limited or constrained by their vision: as the dream or vision grows, so does the possibility of success. A person's seeing depends on the "lens" they look through. Someone correctly observed that, "We don't see things as they are but as we are." You will be what you see, but what you

> *We don't see things as they are but as we are.*

do not see, you cannot be. What you look at lovingly, longingly, and lastingly, you will become like! Your gaze will determine your growth and ultimately whatever you behold you will become.

Claude Monet, the famed French painter, said, "I am the absolute prisoner of my eyes." To a large degree, this is true of every person. Everything begins with perception or "seeing."

Vision is the dominate factor that governs a person's life. Vision determines all the choices you make. It's what your mind naturally gravitates toward when it's not concentrating on something else. It's what your prayers are about. Your vision determines how and where you will spend your money.

But vision alone is not enough to accomplish your dreams. We must "seed" our dreams with the things that carry the pattern for bringing what we see to fruition.

For example, if you "see" yourself in health, then you must "seed" yourself according to the things that make for healthy living. You can see yourself as slim and trim, fit and firm in muscle tone, but if you do not "seed" this vision with healthy eating habits; plenty of exercise and rest; a positive mental attitude, then you will reap only what you sow and not what you see!

If you "see" yourself with lots of friends, then you must "seed" yourself with a friendly attitude and approach to people.

If you "see" yourself as maturing in the Christian faith, then you must "seed" yourself in the ways of discipleship.

If you "see" yourself as prosperous financially, then you must "seed" yourself in the principles of Biblical stewardship over your finances.

If you "see" your business expanding and enriching you and those under you, then you must "seed" yourself with the principles and practices that will reproduce your goals and dreams.

There are countless examples of how differing visions cause different actions (seeding) that produce very different results. Darrow Miller declares in his book "Discipling Nations", the difference "seeing" and "seeding" make in the life of a people: "When studying in Israel at the Institute for Holy Land Studies, I saw a forest unlike any I had seen before. The trees were the same height and planted in rows. When I asked the instructor the cause of this phenomenon, I was told that the Israelis had planted the forest. The instructor continued by explaining two different visions for this land. The Arabs believed that Allah had put a curse on the land. Consequently, they lived at a subsistence level for generations. The Jews believed that Jehovah had said the land would flow with milk and honey. Consequently, they developed one of the most productive arid-land agricultural programs in the world. The natural resources available to both peoples were the same. It was the difference in vision that produced a very different reality." The Jews' vision of the land caused them to take action and seed a forest.

Seeds are mysterious, remarkable things. Their power to multiply, if the laws of the harvest are properly followed, is nothing short of breathtaking and mind-boggling. A case in point is that of a scientist who, in 1968, discovered a 600-year-old seed necklace in a Native American grave. He planted one of the

> *Seed and seeding are the key to success in everything.*

seeds, and it sprouted and grew. Though it had been dormant for 600 years, the potential for life was still there in the seed.

What is it that motivates the farmer to labor tirelessly, sacrifice time and monies, and patiently wait for several weeks or months after he has sown good seed in good soil in the right season? It is the power of the promised, vastly multiplied harvest. He knows that if he plants enough seed to grow 1.4 million plants, (this is about one acre of wheat) his efforts will yield around 77,300,000 kernels! An example of this "seed power" is shown in the statistics from the state of Virginia in 1999, where 260,000 acres of soft red wheat were harvested to produce 14 million bushels or a net worth of approximately $42 million dollars! That same year 60,000 acres of barley were harvested to produce 4.9 million bushels or a net worth of over $8 million.

Seed power is graphically illustrated by the following story: "It has five leaves, stands 14 inches high and is nicknamed Methuselah. It looks like an ordinary date palm seedling, but for UCLA educated botanist Elaine Solowey, it is a piece of history brought back to life.

Planted on Jan. 25, the seedling growing in the black pot in Solowey's nursery on this kibbutz in Israel's Arava desert is 2,000 years old -- more than twice as old as the 900-year-old biblical character who lent his name to the young tree. It is the oldest seed ever known to produce a viable young tree.

The seed that produced Methuselah was discovered during archaeological excavations at King Herod's palace on Mount Masada, near the Dead Sea. Its age has been confirmed by carbon dating." Wow! The latent power in a seed, be it a physical seed or a mental seed, is astounding and should serve to motivate us all to want to be good seed sowers.

All of us are life-farmers in that we have been given the precious gift of life. We have an assignment on earth to fulfill and have access to good and bad seeds with which we can sow and reap much greater blessings or cursings in our lives and in the lives of others for the glory of God. Having been given the precious gift of life, we are to work in a cooperative venture with God in being successful with these talents on loan from Him.

God's view of success is not having it all by way of name, fame, and fortune, but it is knowing how He made us to function consistently within His purpose. Success involves both growing to our full potential within His plan, and sowing seeds from our life into others for the sake of generational transfer. There is no success without a successor.

God Builds on the Principle of the Seed

"Now he who supplies seed to the sower and bread for food will also supply and increase your store of seed and will enlarge the harvest of your righteousness." [1] *"For you have been born again, not of perishable seed, but of imperishable, through the living and enduring word of God."* [2]

The Bible uses the concept of "seed" in a number of ways. For example, Jesus is referred to as the "Seed of the woman." The Word of God is designated as "seed." The proclaiming of the gospel message is likened to the massive scattering of seed. The seed received in good soil produces a vast harvest.[4]

Darrow Miller in commenting on the truth that God builds on the principle of the seed says, "The First Farmer not only planted a garden, but He designed the system -- one simple yet profound, beautiful yet rational. And this system is not a mere mechanical scheme, but a lively work of art and a divine order. At the heart of the divine order is the simple seed. In the creation account, it records that on the third day of creation, God said, *Then he told them many things in parables, saying: "A farmer went out to sow his seed. As he was scattering the seed, some fell along the path, and the birds came and ate it up. Some fell on rocky places, where it did not have much soil. It sprang up quickly, because the soil was shallow. But when the sun came up, the plants were scorched, and they withered because they had no root. Other seed fell among thorns, which grew up and choked the plants. Still other seed fell on good soil, where it produced a crop — a hundred, sixty or thirty times what was sown."*[5]

> *The First Farmer not only planted a garden, but He designed the system.*

'Then God said, "Let the land produce vegetation: seed-bearing plants and trees on the land that bear fruit with seed in it, according to their various kinds." And it was so. The land produced vegetation: plants bearing seed according to their kinds and trees bearing fruit with seed in it according to their kinds. And God saw that it was good.' [6]

From the vast array of the heavens to the miracle of the seed, God created with patterns and textures. Order and beauty were spoken into this lively work of art. Plants and trees are seed bearing. They reproduce life after their design.

There is no place where we see this more profoundly expressed than in the seed. Seeds allow for reproduction, for the expansion of life, for the growing of the garden, for the sending out of culture makers to all the corners of the earth. Imagine if the system of the seed called for only a one for one exchange, one seed would reproduce just one seed. Death would have been built into the system. But the miracle of the seed produces a bountiful garden. From one seed comes a plant that produces many fruit, and within each fruit are many seeds. The agriculturist and horticulturist have the honor of participating in this miracle."

There is a proverb that describes the glory of the seed: "You can count the number of seeds in a apple, but you cannot count the number of apples in a seed." From one seed can come a virtually unlimited harvest that has the potential to perpetuate its self for many generations to come.

Pastor T. D. Jakes writes concerning God's order that operates from the principle of the seed: "Our God is methodical. He is not chaotic. If we want to be prosperous both spiritually and naturally, then we must endeavor to know and function within His divine order. I am reminded of that truth whenever I read about the creation of our world. It is there that God, through His eternal wisdom, whispers in the ear of His servant the unveiled blueprint of the creation of the universe.... It is here that God begins the order from which His methodical structure for all truth

> *Our God is methodical. He is not chaotic.*

emanates and flourishes. For instance, He calls from the muddy montage of an uninhabited planet the herbs, plants, and greenery. He brings forth these plants whose seed will reproduce and grow in the calm summer breezes of thousands of years.

He will create only once the blade of grass which He

expects to garnish His fields. His plan is so futuristic that it puts within each plant a seed of potential. The seed holds the key to reproduction and thereby eliminates the possibility of extinction. Each blade had a destiny created in its origin. Its future is perpetuated in the integrity of its seed. As long as there is a seed to germinate, the blade, through its progeny, will be represented. Its purpose cannot be aborted. It is this principle that governs all of God's creation."

We discover that after the radical destruction of the old world by a flood, God gave to Noah and the other seven whom He had preserved through the cataclysmic judgment the principle of the seed, seedtime and harvest. *"As long as the earth endures, seedtime and harvest, cold and heat, summer and winter, day and night will never cease."* [7]

Getting more personal, your life and mine began by the seed principle and every act of our lives since our births has operated by the seed principle, i.e., sowing and reaping. The principle continues today. You must continually sow by faith the seed of God's Word in the soil of your earthly assignments in order to overcome life's problems and reach your potential in life; to see your life become fruitful and replenished in health; to manage your family and your finances; and to grow in your spiritual life.

Successful life farming necessitates coming to a better understanding of the principle in the Word of God -- the Law of Reciprocity -- better known as the Law of Sowing and Reaping. In physics, it is called the law of "cause and effect" or "for every action there is an equal and opposite reaction;" in finance, it is called the law of "investment and return;" in theology, it is referred to as the law of "giving and receiving." The farmer would call this law the principle of "planting and harvesting." The simple man on the street may refer to it as, "what goes around comes around" or "one good turn deserves another."

Stephen Covey, author of *The Seven Habits of Highly Effective People*, refers to this principle by using the phrase "emotional bank account" to describe the principle of reciprocity and the corresponding credit-withdrawal process in relationships. Using the metaphor of a financial bank account, the emotional bank account describes the trust that accumulates in a relationship. Like the financial bank account, you must make deposits before you can make withdrawals.

If you were to share one negative word, there is not just one negative result. The repercussions of that action are much greater because that one negative seed has the power to cause multiple results. There is a story told of two people who were in a quarrel. One person was very unkind with his words. After a short period of time, the offender was convicted and went to ask forgiveness. In response, the offended party said, "You are forgiven, but there is still hurt. Take a feather pillow downtown on this windy afternoon and empty its contents into the wind. After you gather all the feathers back into the pillow, only then, will my pain be gone."

> *It is imperative that we continue to make deposits of positive words and deeds into the accounts of lives around us.*

Years ago in our marriage seminar, Billie and I shared about how love tanks are to be filled to have the maximum impact in your marriage. This is no different than having a full emotional bank account. We have a tendency to be unkind with our words and deeds which drains our accounts. It is imperative that we continue to make deposits of positive words and deeds into the accounts of the lives around us. Like the empty feather pillow, once the words are spoken, once the unkindness is done, once the slander hits the four winds, it is impossible to gather back all the damage that has been done.

In every use, this law or principle requires a costly and consistent sowing process that will produce some sort of harvest, either good or bad and this in abundance or scarcity.

All individuals in every generation cooperate in the fulfilling or failing to fulfill their own destiny by their response to God's Seed.

Most people are familiar with the nursery rhyme that asks and answers a question about a garden:

Mary, Mary quite contrary,
How does your garden grow?
With silver bells and cockle shells
And pretty maids all in a row.

What most people do not know is the origin and meaning of this nursery rhyme. It originated from England and the "Mary" referred to is Mary Tudor, or Bloody Mary, who was the daughter of King Henry VIII. Queen Mary was a staunch Catholic and the garden referred to is an allusion to graveyards which were increasing in size with those who dared to continue to adhere to the Protestant faith. The silver bells and cockle shells were colloquialisms for instruments of torture. The 'maids' were a device to behead people similar to the guillotine.

Queen Mary sowed bad seed in her garden and the evil effects of religious strife and hatred are still being reaped to this very day. These are historical facts. That is why we must sow Godly seed for future generations. Religion doesn't stop hatred. One man has said, "You can know for sure that you have created God in your own image when it turns out that He hates the same people you hate."

The Word of God, with the promises, provisions and purposes it contains comes to us in the form of seed that requires a planting in our hearts by faith. What was seed that developed into fruit in one person must be received as seed that has the potential to become fruit for you.

Seeding Principle #1 -- A Seed, until it is Planted in Good Soil, is only the Promise of Future Potential

"I tell you the truth, unless a kernel of wheat falls to the ground and dies, it remains only a single seed. But if it dies, it produces many seeds." [8]

We need to change the manner in which we view the powerful potential in both good and bad seed. If you were standing before me and I opened my hand and showed you an apple seed, there would be two ways of viewing the seed – practically and potentially. Practically, you would see a single seed from a fruit we call an apple. Potentially, you would see a whole orchard of apple trees latent in the seed! Remember the aforementioned proverb: "You can count the

> *We need to change the manner in which we view the powerful potential in good and bad seeds.*

number of seeds in an apple, but you cannot count the number of apples in a seed." Someone aptly said, "An orchard of apple trees in this narrow shell we call a seed is contained; here in its safe and simple house of death, sealed in its shell a million apples leap; here I can blow an orchard with my breath and in my hand an orchard lies asleep."

Seed-Power is an awesome, astounding, and mind-boggling thing! A seed is a living pattern, a genetically coded structure that under the right circumstances will reproduce its parent, with unity in diversity. A good seed is a word, a pattern, a vision, a picture or an idea for changing creation to conform to God's design. In contrast, a bad seed is a word, a pattern, a vision, a picture or an idea for changing creation to continued rebellion against God's design.

Think of what incredible potential rests in each human life when Jesus (the Seed of God; the life-principle) is resident there! But what if Jesus is only resident and not released; contained, concealed and confined there? Then, we abide tragically "alone."

Seeding Principle # 2 --The Power of the Seed in Growth Potential isn't Equal to the Size of the Seed

In my book, "Sequoia Size Success," I discuss this principle: the power of the seed in growth. The giant sequoia trees have survived for two or three thousand years. A case in point of the above principle is that of the giant sequoia tree, which grows on the western side of the Sierra Nevada Mountains in 75 groves in an area 260 miles long and 15 miles wide. These trees have survived for two or three thousand years, some even longer. Some of the largest of these trees measure 45 feet in base diameter and up to 300 feet in height, with their bark being sometimes as much as 4 feet thick, with 50 foot long branches that begin some 100 feet up on the tree. The tallest standing giant sequoia is 311 feet tall. The Sequoias are nature's tallest and oldest living things, yet they came from a cone about the size of a chicken egg and the seeds from these cones are only the size of a flake of oatmeal!

There is not a correlation between the size of the seed and its power for growth. In today's world, this principle is ignored or forgotten. We live in times in which if anything or anyone starts out small or few, it is considered laughable and is disparaged. If it isn't massive in numbers, mighty in influence; if it isn't big, beautiful (and brawny); if it isn't large, loud and lauded by the masses-it isn't considered worthwhile.

Have you noticed how very few people are willing to start where they are with what they have? Instead they wind up either never doing anything because they cannot begin big and powerful or they play to the crowd and start up with an impressive show, the big venture, the spectacular splash, only to fizzle in the end. They want to capture the attention and admiration of as many people as possible as quickly as possible. This is the American way for the most part, but it is not God's way. He begins everything He does in a small way; with a

> *Have you noticed how very few people are willing to start where they are with what they have?*

seed, an idea, a word; a baby, sub-atomic particles, atoms, etc. In proper cooperation with His design and His laws, growth, increase and steady progress come to fruition.

Jesus, in encouraging His disciples not to be discouraged because of the apparent smallness of the seed of the kingdom message, declares, *"Again he said, 'What shall we say the kingdom of God is like, or what parable shall we use to describe it? It is like a mustard seed, which is the smallest seed you plant in the ground. Yet when planted, it grows and becomes the largest of all garden plants, with such big branches that the birds of the air can perch in its shade.'"* [9]

In that same teaching, Jesus stated this principle again as He said, *"The kingdom of heaven is like yeast that a woman took and mixed into a large amount of flour until it worked all through the dough."* [10] Jesus reveals in this parable of the kingdom that there is a process at work in the Kingdom of God that produces an end product that is far in excess of natural expectations. Three "satas" of flour is enough to make bread for around 100 persons. For a housewife in New Testament times, before the days of refrigeration, to bake in these amounts for her household was unthinkable.

In this parable, yeast represents the positive, powerful, penetrating influence of the kingdom message as expressed through the lives of the redeemed. The power of the king-

> *What seems so insignificant to the world has the potential to impact the whole world.*

dom works imperviously – it's hidden in the flour; it works powerfully – leavening the whole; and it works persistently.

Charles Spurgeon encouraged a gathering of missionaries with these words: "I myself believe that King Jesus will reign, and all idols will be utterly abolished; but I expect the same power which turned the world upside down once will still continue to do it. The Holy Spirit would never suffer the Word of God to rest upon His holy name if He was not able to convert the world."

This is what the Father promised His Son, in planning the Covenant of Redemption: *"It is too small a thing for you to be my servant to restore the tribes of Jacob and bring back those of Israel I have kept. I will also make you a light for the Gentiles, that you may bring my salvation to the ends of the earth."* [11]

From such insignificant beginnings – twelve men, personally trained and empowered by the Lord Jesus -- the seed of the sons and daughters of the kingdom, sowing the word of the kingdom of God has multiplied until one of every ten people on the planet is of the Bible-reading, Bible-believing stream of Christianity. The number of believers in what used to be "mission fields" now surpasses the number of believers in the countries from which missionaries were originally sent. In fact, more missionaries are now sent from non-Western churches than from the traditional mission-sending bases in the West. The Protestant growth rate in Latin America is well over three times the biological growth rate. Protestants in China grew from about 50,000 to somewhere between 63 and 83 million believers in less than 50 years, with most of that growth occurring in just the last few decades.

In the late 1980s, Isaac Kim took one Bible to a village in northeast China. When he returned a few years later, there were ten thousand converts – all saying it was because of the one Bible he had brought.

Truly, there is wonder-working power in the "Seed of the Word of God!"

What You Seed is What You Get!

Good Seed brought to reproductive maturity and ongoing good seeding is the key to being a successful life-farmer!

Seeding Principle # 3 --Seed Comes from Previous Seed, thus we are always Reaping where we haven't Sown!

Solomon wrote, "*Cast your bread upon the waters, for after many days you will find it again. Give portions to seven, yes to eight, for you do not know what disaster may come upon the land. If clouds are full of water, they pour rain upon the earth. Whether a tree falls to the south or to the north, in the place where it falls, there will it lie. Whoever watches the wind will not plant; whoever looks at the clouds will not reap. As you do not know the path of the wind, or how the body is formed in a mother's womb, so you cannot understand the work of God, the Maker of all things. Sow your seed in the morning, and at evening let not your hands be idle, for you do not know which will succeed, whether this or that, or whether both will do equally well.*" [12]

As we give generously, we will at times give to people who will never personally give back to us. These individuals who we seeded into will seed into others. Scripture does not say that we will receive from the source where

When you cast your bread upon the water, it will come back to you.

we sowed, but it does say that we will receive a return later. It is possible to receive from a different source than where you have sown. It is not up to you to determine where you will reap the harvest; just know that there will be a harvest. When you cast your bread upon the water, it will come back to you.

Remember that God is your source, not people. God may use people; and who God uses is His prerogative. Always remember that God is the source.

Jesus informed His disciples that their current success in ministry was due to the previous generation's faithful sowing, even though they did not get to reap very much of the harvest: *"I sent you to reap what you have not worked for. Others have done the hard work, and you have reaped the benefits of their labor."* [13] What does it matter who gets the credit, as long as God gets the glory and people get the help?

Reaping a harvest or success is not measured in terms of prosperity, power, prominence or popularity. It is not measured in terms of what or how many things we have reaped or accumulated, but by the level of our obedience to the assignment to go on sowing good seeds, irrespective of the apparent success or failure of our efforts!

Success is determined by God!
Outcome is determined by God!

We need to define success Biblically. Success to the world generally means results. As far as the kingdom of God goes, success has less to do with results than it does faithfulness. God requires that we be faithful as a steward and one day God will say, *"Well done, good and faithful servant! You have been faithful with a few things; I will put you in charge of many things. Come and share your master's happiness!"* [14] Success is determined by God. Outcome is determined by God. Results are determined by God. Faithfulness is determined by us.

Results are determined by God!
Faithfulness is determined by us!

21

What You Seed is What You Get!

The foundational truth of the Laws of the Harvest is that no one can reap until someone has sown. Life always comes from previous life. There is no such thing as a spontaneous generation. Spiritually and materially speaking, blessings come from those who sowed good seed and curses come from sowing bad seed.

It is absolutely imperative that we sow good seeds for future generations so that they do not have to start from scratch. If we continue to reap a good seed harvest to meet only our needs without sowing good seeds in return, we borrow from someone else's harvest, and sow bad seeds of greed and selfishness for the future.

Seed Sowing Principle # 4 --The Seed You Have Been Given Must be Sown in Faith to Obtain What You Have Been Promised

It was a custom of the ancient Egyptians to place seeds in the hands of those they buried. When archeologists discovered and opened some of those tombs that had been undisturbed for four thousand years, there was not one more grain than had been originally buried. And yet agricultural authorities tell us that if one of those grains that had been sealed in a tomb for thousands of years had fallen into the ground and died, in twenty years' time its normal increase would equal all the wheat crops of the world. The life was there, but it was contained, confined, concealed, imprisoned, and unproductive. You see, you may polish or paint the seed, shine it and enshrine it, and protect it by placing it carefully on a safe shelf, but if you do, it will remain "alone."

May the Spirit of the Living God open our eyes to begin to see more clearly what limitless potential there is in one person in whom the "life-germ" -- Jesus Christ -- dwells. How essential it is, then, that we discover the meaning of these spiritual laws of sowing and reaping. Let's ask God to give us the grace, love and wisdom to choose daily to order our lives by them. This way we sow copiously into the lives of others and bring glory to our God.

Dennis Waitley illustrates the importance of consistently sowing good seed even when it appears that there is nothing to be gained from it. "On a stormy night many years ago, an elderly couple entered a hotel lobby and asked for a room.

"I'm very sorry," responded the night clerk. "We are completely full with a convention group. Normally, I would send you to another hotel that we use for our overflow in situations like this, but I know they, too, are full."

He paused for a moment and then went on, "On a night like tonight, I can't imagine sending you out in this weather again. It may not be a luxury suite, but you can stay in my room. It's clean, and I'll stay here and finish up some book work in the office since the regular night auditor won't be coming in."

The distinguished-looking man and woman appeared uncomfortable at inconveniencing the clerk in this way but graciously accepted his offer of hospitality. When the man came down to pay his bill the next morning, the clerk was still at the desk. He said, "Oh, there will be no charge for the room. I live here full-time so I can put in as many hours as possible to earn a little extra. The room is already taken care of."

The older man said, "You're the kind of person every hotel owner dreams of having as an employee. Maybe someday I'll build a hotel for you."

The young hotel clerk was flattered, but the idea sounded so outrageous that he chuckled at the elderly man's joke after the couple had departed.

A few years passed, and one day the hotel clerk, still at the same job and place, received a registered letter from the elderly man. His comments reflected his vivid recollection of that stormy night. He invited the hotel clerk to visit him in New York and enclosed a round-trip ticket in the letter.

Arriving a few days later in Manhattan, the clerk was met by his admirer at the corner of Fifth Avenue and Thirty-Fourth Street where a magnificent new building stood.

"That," explained the elderly man, "is the hotel I have built for you to run. I told you at the time it might happen."

"You can't be serious," said the clerk. "What's the catch? Why me? Who are you anyway?" stammered the flustered young man. The gentleman smiled, "My name is William Waldorf Astor. And there's no catch. You are the person I want to run this hotel."

That hotel was the original Waldorf-Astoria, and the clerk who accepted the first managerial position was George Boldt.

Seeding Principle #5 -- Sowing Seed Places Us in a Helpless, but not Hopeless Position that Requires T.N.T.

"He also said, "This is what the kingdom of God is like. A man scatters seed on the ground. Night and day, whether he sleeps or gets up, the seed sprouts and grows, though he does not know how. All by itself the soil produces grain — first the stalk, then the head, then the full kernel in the head. As soon as the grain is ripe, he puts the sickle to it, because the harvest has come." 15

Jesus said, *"I tell you the truth, unless a kernel of wheat falls to the ground and dies, it remains only a single seed. But if it dies, it produces many seeds. The man who loves his life will lose it, while the man who hates his life in this world will keep it for eternal life."* 16 What I believe Christ is saying among other things is when a grain of wheat is planted and dies four things happen: 1) The grain disappears. 2) The grain deteriorates. 3) The grain disintegrates; and 4) the grain is destroyed.

But the good news is that only after this takes place can that grain of wheat, or your life, produce a great harvest.

T.N.T. stands for time, nurturing, and tenacity. The principle of sowing, during the germination time, places us in a very helpless condition, but proper nurturing and a tenacious attitude that believes good seed sown in good soil will eventually rise above its earthly tomb and demonstrate fruitfulness of life. Some seeds grow easily and quickly while others take time. A dandelion grows overnight while asparagus takes two years. A fungus, like a mushroom, grows overnight while an oak tree takes many years. In emphasizing the importance of tenacity in the process of implementing the laws of the harvest, someone said that a great oak tree is but a little nut that stood its ground!

What You Seed is What You Get!

Seeding Principle #6 -- When You Want a Harvest You've Never Had, You've got to Start Sowing Seed that You've Never Sown!

The point is this: *"...Whoever sows sparingly will also reap sparingly, and whoever sows generously will also reap generously."* [17]

You must start where you are with the seed you have, and not sit around waiting for the flowers to arrive. You must start now and sow bountifully and sacrificially. Stop looking at the size of the need and begin to see the potential in the seed! You establish your harvest size when and how you sow your seed, so you must always sow to your harvest size and not from your harvest size.

> *Stop looking at the size of the need and begin to see the potential in the seed!*

Gary Carpenter gives a personal testimony of this principle. Although it is somewhat lengthy, I have taken the liberty to include it in its entirety because it so convincingly illustrates principle number six.

"The Holy Spirit got very personal with me and said, 'Gary, I have blessed the only field that you have sown in the earth as much as is possible. I am speaking of your job. If I am going to increase your material harvest financially, you are going to have to sow into some larger fields IN THE EARTH.

> *Talk about your future, not your failures.*

Normally, most people have sown only a very small field,

26

usually a simple job. God can bless that field to the maximum until every square inch has a stalk of corn growing up in it, but if that field is small (small growth potential), then you are not going to see much difference in his prosperity compared to his neighbor.

In my case, I was still working as a driver for Crane Carrier when the Holy Spirit taught me this lesson. The first year I worked at Crane Carrier I made about $26,000.00. Five years later, when the Holy Spirit spoke this to me, I was making about $40,000.00, but that was the maximum harvest potential from that field. There was no more room for growth. It was maxed out.

To get a larger material harvest I was going to have to fence in larger fields either by acquiring more marketable skills to obtain

If all you do is all you're doing, all you'll get is all you're getting.

a better job, sowing into stocks, bonds, or other investments, etc. I had to somehow sow more ground in order for God to be able to pour down His blessing on it and give me a larger harvest.

GOD HAS RAINED HIS FAVOR UPON THIS WHOLE NATION! AS A NATION, WE HAVE WHAT WE NEED FOR ABUNDANCE! GOD HAS DONE HIS PART! So what is it that is limiting your individual harvest? THE SIZE OF THE FIELD YOU HAVE DECIDED TO SOW IN THE EARTH!

For example, a high school dropout who has no skills other than manual labor has limited the field that he can sow into. Perhaps the largest field he can work in is capped by a wage of say $6.00 per hour. Here is the promise of Malachi to that man. God will rain favor upon that man to the point that his 'field' is wall to wall corn. In this case, that means the man would rise from the minimum wage to earning the maximum potential of $6.00 per hour. Once the man is making the top dollar for that job, GOD HAS DONE HIS PART! If the man wants a larger harvest than that, he is going to have to SOW INTO A LARGER FIELD!

That normally means acquiring additional skills. I am speaking of such things as technical school, reading, writing, arithmetic, computer skills, marketing, SOMETHING! GOD DOES NOT BLESS INCOMPETENCE! GOD DOES NOT BLESS IGNORANCE! He is not going to exalt you beyond your level of competence. Put very plainly, God is not going to promote you to be the head of General Motors Corporation if you are not qualified for the job.

Jesus said, 'The laborer is worthy of his hire.' What does that mean? God will see to it that you are paid in proportion to your labor, but it also means that God is not going to have an employer pay you $100 per hour to flip hamburgers at McDonald's.

God is pouring the rain of His favor upon you every day. The main thing limiting your prosperity is the size of the field you are sowing into. If you want to harvest from larger fields, then you are most likely going to have to acquire some additional skills that God can bless. This part is not fun. It requires effort. It means burning the midnight oil after you have already put in a full day's work."

We tend to let our time manage us and not manage our time. Time has been given to us by God to use wisely. Every man and woman has the same twenty four hours in the day.

Why do some people get more done in their day? They have learned the principle of seizing the day. The day of opportunity is upon us. We must maximize our moments. Use time; don't abuse time. Often you may hear the response, "I'm just burning time." Don't

> We tend to let our time manage us and not manage our time.

be caught using this statement when asked, "What are you doing?" Make every moment count. You only have a few.

Remember, when you want a harvest you have never had, you have got to start sowing seed that you have never sown! Brian Tracy said, "If all you do is all you're doing, all you'll get is all you're getting."

Years ago when the Lord allowed me to become acquainted with World Wide Dream Builders, I realized that there were entrepreneurs in this organization who were willing to seed their way to success. The opportunities are unlimited. The organization of World Wide is one of the greatest support systems that I have ever seen anywhere. I recognize that there are many people in the organization who are unwilling to pay the price for their success. No matter how great the system, no matter how great the tools, no matter how encouraging the leaders, some people are unwilling to seed their way to success. Opportunities can be there. The need can be there. Even the desire can be there, but without seed-

> Many are unwilling to pay the price for success.

ing, without discipline, without change, there will not be a future harvest. The reason I admire these leaders in World Wide Dream Builders so greatly and what they are trying to provide for the whole organization is that they have been willing to pay the price to change through hard work and through discipline to set an example for all those who come behind them. Everybody has the same opportunity. Everybody can be successful from God's perspective if they are willing to do all that God mandates them to do in seed-time and harvest.

The Principle of "Seeding" where you are going involves:

Seeding appropriately.

If we sow bad seed, it will without exception produce a bad harvest. In contrast, good seed must be sown in the appropriate season and soil. Even the best of seed, if left alone after sowing, will produce a bad or very poor harvest.

Seeds we receive into our hearts and minds conceive a belief system. The offspring of this conception produces seed thoughts. If allowed to germinate and come to fruition, the thoughts sown will produce attitudes. Attitudes sown will produce actions. Actions repeatedly sown will produce a habit or a lifestyle. Habits sown will produce character. Character sown will reap a destiny.

Weeding thoroughly and feeding properly.

Weeding and feeding is essential to achieving a successful harvest both in the literal fields of agriculture and in our lives.

Weeding means plucking out of your life things that compete with the new life that is developing within you, lest it choke out or severely diminish the health and fruitfulness of the good seed plant.

Proper weeding requires that we have readily available a "file 13", e.g. a "waste basket", so that all the junk and bulk delivery type things that come our way in life can be quickly disposed before collecting, cluttering, and choking out the space needed for "good seed" plants to thrive.

A caveat in respect to weeding is given in a parable by Jesus: *"The kingdom of heaven is like a man who sowed good seed in his field. But while everyone was sleeping, his enemy came and sowed weeds among the wheat, and went away. When the wheat sprouted and formed heads, then the weeds also appeared. The owner's servants came to him and said, 'Sir, didn't you sow good seed in your field? Where then did the weeds come from?' 'An enemy did this,' he replied. The servants asked him, 'Do you want us to go and pull them up?' 'No,' he answered, 'because while you are pulling the weeds, you may root up the wheat with them. Let both grow together until the harvest. At that time I will tell the harvesters: First collect the weeds and tie them in bundles to be burned; then gather the wheat and bring it into my barn.'"* [18]

The warning of this parable is not to set yourself up as a little god. Don't try to rid life of all those who are posing as wheat

> *Don't forget that we are called to be wheat growers and not just weed-pullers!*

when in reality they are weeds. Let's personalize this principle. Let's not become absorbed with trying to get rid of all the weeds in our life, or we will become weed, or bad-seed focused. We should be good-seed focused. If we only focus on eliminating weed we destroy the good seed that by far outnumbers the bad. In other words, don't forget that we are called to be wheat growers and not just weed-pullers!

What You Seed is What You Get!

Of course, the main thing is to feed with proper nutrients the growing crop, so that we reap a great harvest. This means when you see signs of success in your labors, feed it, cultivate it, and create more room for growth.

The harvest that you anticipate corresponds with the seed that is being sown. Remember that this principle requires a costly and consistent sowing process which will produce some sort of harvest, either good or bad, in abundance or scarcity. Think on these positives and negatives and the ramifications of both.

Seeds	Harvests
Kindness	Friendships
Compassion	Love
Generosity	Abundance
Faith	Courage
Storms of Life	Patience
Trust	Peace
Discipline	Order
Attitude	Achievement
Meekness	Power
Mercy	Respect

Sowing Principle #7 -- Judge Each Day, Not by the Harvest You're Reaping, but by the Seed You're Sowing!

"Let us not become weary in doing good, for at the proper time we will reap a harvest if we do not give up." [19]

The Laws of the Harvest are perhaps the easiest to understand and the easiest to ignore! We must continually "seed" the future we "see" with the types of ideas, words, visions, or pictures needed for this changing creation to conform to God's design. If we fail to do this, we will be consumers and not reproducers; reapers and not sowers; getters and not givers. We will soon exhaust the harvest.

We are not good life-farmers if we merely sow a bunch of seeds on occasion. Good life-farmers sow consistently and plan for the future. The only control that we have over the nature of our future is conditioned by the type of seed we are sowing and the willingness to go on sowing for future generations so that they do not have to start from the bottom of an empty seed barrel.

Mike Murdock recommends that, "If what you have isn't big enough to be your harvest, make it your seed, because that seed is the only influence you have over the future." Another way to put that would be, "When what you have won't meet your need, use it as seed."

> *"When what you have won't meet your need, use it as seed."*

Far too often we see people reap a bad harvest because they considered the immediate cost of changing sowing patterns and deemed them too expensive or inconvenient to change. This outlook produces a harvest much like that of the people in a town in northwest Turkey that suffered great loss of people and property in the 1999 earthquake. In 1969, thirty years before the quake, one of the small towns in that region had been warned by the authorities that the town was situated right on top of a major fault line. The danger was so significant that they urged them to relocate the entire community as quickly as possible.

The citizens gathered to discuss the issue. The town council, due to the costly sacrifices and inconvenience of relocating, voted unanimously to redraw the map and move the fault line on the map rather than move the town! As a result of the seed sown by a few, many paid with their lives, and all paid with the loss of their homes! Too costly—too inconvenient. We keep redrawing the map of our life to accommodate these two excuses. The result is devastation. Quit redrawing the map. Heed the warnings and plant the right seed in the right soil for the right reason and you will have the right results.

Where Do You "Seed" Yourself Going?

Where you "see" yourself a few years from now will become a reality because you are "seeding" the good seed, presently and persistently, that carries the DNA that will produce the harvest you have seen.

Chapter Two:
Seeding under the Law of Compound Interest!

Succeeding in life should be spelled SUC-SEED–ING. Without clearly understanding and consistently cooperating with the laws of the harvest, we are destined to failure. Professor John Lawrence spoke accurately when he said, "If the farmer knew no more about the principles of farming than the average Christian does about producing a spiritual harvest, he would never make it through the winter."

One of the laws or principles of successful life farming is that of "spiritual compound interest." This principle can be stated as: "We reap not only what we sow, but far more than we sow!"

In the parable of the sower, the seed, and the soils, Jesus reveals the impact of this aspect of the laws of the harvest when He declares that the successful sowing of the seeds produces a harvest varying from 30, 60, to 100-fold. By the way, an hundred fold is 10,000 percent interest on one's investment! At the end of this chapter, the interpretation of this passage will be explained in greater depth.

What You Seed is What You Get!

Compound interest is considered one of the great miracles of all of human history and economics. No wonder Nathan Rothschild declared that, "compound interest should be the 8th wonder of the world." Albert Einstein described it as the most powerful force in our society.

We reap not only what we sow, but far more than we sow!

In order to assist you to wrap your mind around this principle, consider the results if your grandfather, about six generations ago, in 1776 had invested $1,000 dollars at 5% interest, compounded annually, with no monies withdrawn. Today (2006), 229 years later, you would have 71 million, 177 thousand 607 dollars and forty-seven cents!

Here's another astounding illustration of the power of compound interest at work. If given the choice to work for me for one month (31 days) for a million dollars or for 1 penny a day, and have that penny doubled each day, which would you choose? Well, at the end of the first week your paycheck would be $0.64 cents! However at the end of 31 days, it would be $10,737,418.24! It's amazing that this could be true; I didn't really believe this when I read it, so I did this by long hand and guess what? It is right.

In the early 1600s, the Native Americans sold an island, now called Manhattan in New York, for various beads and trinkets worth about $24. Since Manhattan real estate is now some of the most expensive in the world, it would seem at first glance that the Native Americans made a terrible deal. Had the Native Americans, however, sold their beads and trinkets, invested their $24 and received 5% compounded annual interest, they might have had enough money to buy back all of Manhattan. The $24 paid by the Dutch to the local Indians for Manhattan Island, if it had been invested at 5% interest for the last 375 years, would today be worth $2,119,329,034.89 dollars.

The power of compound interest is nothing more than the principle of the law of the harvest that declares: "We reap not only what we sow, but far, far, far, more than we sow!"

Successful "Seeding" Under the Law of Compound Interest Requires Knowing that the Only Preparation for Tomorrow is the Right Use of Today

Charlie Brown is seen at bat. "STRIKE THREE!" He has struck out again and slumps down on the players' bench. He says, "Rats! I'll never be a big league player. I just don't have it! All my life I've dreamed of playing in the big leagues, but I know I'll never make it."

Lucy turns to console him. "Charlie Brown, you're think-ing too far ahead. What you

> *The first step toward a great harvest is the step you make today!*

need to do is set yourself more immediate goals."

Charlie Brown looks up and asks, "Immediate goals?" Lucy responds, "Yes. Start with this next inning when you go out to pitch. See if you can walk out to the mound without falling down."

The first step toward a great harvest is the step you make today. Make it forward, godly, well aimed, and purposeful. Take the best seed, with the right purpose, and start sowing it in the soil that will produce the harvest that God has designed for you. Remember, the steps you take today become the well-worn path of tomorrow.

Take the Risk of Investing in the Lives of Others Through Generous Distribution

"Cast your bread upon the waters, for after many days you will find it again." [1]

We are admonished to "cast our bread upon the waters for you will find it after many days." Scholars are not exactly sure what Solomon meant by this expression. Some suggest that he meant investing wisely in the import--export shipping business. Others suggest that Solomon borrowed from a happening that took place in Egypt at the flooding of the Nile. After the Nile overflowed its banks and began to recede, there would be a small amount of water left in the low lying areas. Men would cast their seed upon the water covering this portion of their fields and as the waters continued to recede into the ground it would carry the seed with it. Thus, the crop just kind of planted itself.

Using a modern idiom, it takes bread, i.e., money or capital to make an investment in a new business venture. Making practical application of this expression would mean, whatever else bread stands for it represents SEED -- that seed includes myself, all that I am, all that I possess. It is also the Word of the Kingdom of God, which represents the will of God. So, what the wise man is admonishing us is to avoid putting the bread in the deep freeze, or hiding it on the shelf, or keeping it sitting on the couch at home, or in the pew at the meetinghouse. Instead, dispense it, distribute it, cast it forth, and sow it. There is to be a generous distribution. We are to be generously investing in the lives of other people

> *Remember, sowing seed is always a risky venture. Those who don't take chances don't make advances!*

for the purpose of seeing His kingdom come more fully in their lives!

Stretch Your Faith by Extending, with Great Diversification, Your Seed-sowing

"Give portions to seven, yes to eight, for you do not know what disaster may come upon the land." [2]

When King Solomon admonishes us to give a portion to seven or eight, he means that we are to do as much good to as many as we can and then some. Also, he is advising us to employ not only generous distribution, but great diversification. Another possible interpretation would be "do not put all your eggs in one basket." You can apply that to the world of investment finance. If you put all of your investments in one venture and it fails, then you have lost everything. You can apply it to domestic and personal relationships. If you spend all your life focusing all your attention upon one person, then if you lose that person, you are left without a friend.

Do you know that most people center their life around one or two persons? It's great to be head-over-heels in love with your mate, and that is the way it should be, but you had better make more friends than just your mate because the time may come when your spouse will be gone before you. Life can be very lonely without friends and without family. That's why Billie and I are so big on friends and family.

Jesus says: *"Give, and it will be given to you. A good measure, pressed down, shaken together and running over, will be poured into your lap. For with the measure you use, it will be measured to you."* [3] Don't miss that last phrase. The return we receive is directly proportional to the measure we use in sharing and investing in the lives of others. Many of us would like to reap an abundant harvest of friends, of good relationships with our families, or with our mates. But our reality is far from a life of abundance. We expect to use a little measure and get back a whole lot in return.

"Remember this: Whoever sows sparingly will also reap sparingly, and whoever sows generously will also reap generously." [4] This truth applies to all areas of life. If you are having a harvest problem, you need to check up on your sowing. If you do not show yourself friendly, you can't expect to have friends. If you are not constantly giving love, you can't expect to receive love. If you are not doing something to cultivate and improve the relationship with your mate, you can't expect to receive a measure in return. With what measure you use, it will be measured back to you.

We are to be casting our bread upon the waters. Be bold! Be willing to take the risk! Anytime you involve yourself with other people, there is going to be the risk of

> *If you are having a harvest problem, you need to check up on your sowing.*

being hurt and rejected. However, we are to take the risk, make ourselves vulnerable and become involved in investing in the lives of others.

Cast your bread, even upon unkindly soil, in unpromising situations. Do it liberally, constantly, and confidently with the firm, settled persuasion that eventually it will come back.[5]

We Must Resist the Tendency to do Nothing for Fear of the Future or of Failure

"If clouds are full of water, they pour rain upon the earth. Whether a tree falls to the south or to the north, in the place where it falls, there will it lie. Whoever watches the wind will not plant; whoever looks at the clouds will not reap " [6]

Spiritual Compound Interest Principle # 1 -- Do not focus on the inevitable

Clouds, rain, fallen trees, etc., are things that happen all the time. So perhaps Solomon meant that certain things are inevitable. Into every life clouds will come, trees will fall, and rain will pour. Even if your efforts are diligent, there is no guarantee bad things won't happen to you. God never said that only good comes your way. He says that He is able to take the good and the bad and mix them together and make everything work ultimately for your good. He does not say everything is good within itself.

This passage also warns us about focusing all our attention upon the potential for rain, clouds, and fallen trees. Instead of sowing, you worry. You can work yourself into such a frenzied state that you paralyze yourself, rendering yourself ineffective. Moreover, you can think and think about the future, hoping to ward off a negative situation. Life is full of unknowns. Despite all your worry and calculation,

God never said that everything good comes your way.

something you did not plan for may arise and totally alter the situation. All that thinking would be for naught.

Chuck Swindoll tells of a man in Belfast, Ireland, during those fearful, terror-filled times who had to be out on the streets after dark. He was thinking about how he was going to get home without getting his throat cut. Slowly and carefully he picked his way along the street and lo and behold the worst of what he expected happened. Some shadowy figure jumped out from behind the corner of a building and grabbed him by the neck and stuck a long knife to his throat and said, "Answer me quickly, are you a Catholic or a Protestant?" Well, he thought very quickly, "If I say I'm a Catholic and he is a Protestant; or if I say I'm a Protestant and he is a Catholic, either way I am a goner." So in a flash of brilliance he blurted out, "I'm a Jew!" The fellow who had the knife to his throat said, "Ha!, I'm the luckiest Arab terrorist in all of Belfast."

Sometimes, in spite of our wisdom, our answers, our adroitness in planning or our best efforts, things still do not work out. Therefore, do not focus on the inevitable, the unpredictable, and the what-if-events of life.

Spiritual Compound Interest Principle # 2--
Do not fear the inauspicious (the unpromising)

Solomon warns: "He who observes the wind will not sow, he who regards the clouds will not reap." One paraphrase says, "If you wait until the wind and the weather are just right, you will never plant anything and never harvest anything." The Living Bible's paraphrase of this verse says, "If you wait for perfect conditions, you will never get anything done."

Solomon is warning us not to wait for ideal conditions before we start to invest in life, and in the lives of others.

Here are some seeds that are worth putting in your life and sowing daily:

A Chinese proverb interprets Solomon's advice by stating that, "Man who waits for roast duck to fly into mouth must wait very, very, long time."

Thomas Edison said, "Opportunity is missed by most people because it is dressed in overalls and looks like work."

Napoleon Hill warns, "Don't wait. The time will never be just right."

William James writes, "There is no more miserable human being than the one in whom nothing is habitual but indecision."

"In any moment of decision, the best thing you can do is the right thing. The worst thing you can do is nothing." - Theodore Roosevelt

"You don't have to be great to get started, but you have to get started to be great." -- Les Brown

"Many people die with their music still in them. Why is this so? Too often it is because they are always getting ready to live. Before they know it, time runs out." -- Oliver Wendell Holmes, Former U.S. Supreme Court Justice

"When it comes to really paying the price for success, some people stop at nothing; that's exactly what they get... nothing."—Paul Tsika

Today is the first day of the rest of your life, don't waste it by living in the "what ifs" or the "it might" outlook. Take the risk! Get involved! Indecision and delay are the parents of failure. Don't wait for the kids to grow up, or until you have more time, more money, a bigger house, or until retirement, to begin to sow toward the harvest of your dreams. We are not suggesting that you spend your life in self-centered pursuits. This is not an admonition to cast it all to the wind, forget about safety, and never save wisely. The point of this verse is, if you are ever going to invest in someone's life, if you are ever going to build your business and develop marketable skills, don't wait until the perfect time -- it does not come in this life. Do it now!

Tucked away in our subconscious is an idyllic vision. We see ourselves on a long trip that spans the continent. We are traveling by train. Through windows we drink in the passing scene of cars on nearby highways, of children waving at a crossing, of cattle grazing on a distant hillside, of smoke pouring from a power plant, of row upon row of corn and wheat, of flatlands and valleys, of mountains and rolling hillsides, of city skylines and village halls. But uppermost in our minds is the final destination. On a certain day at a certain hour, we will pull into the station. Bands will be playing and flags waving. Once we get there so many wonderful dreams will come true and the pieces of our lives will fit together like a completed jigsaw puzzle. How restlessly we pace the aisles, waiting, waiting, waiting. "When we reach the station, that will be it!" we cry. "When I am 18." "When I buy a new 450 SL Mercedes Benz!" "When I put the last kid through college." "When I have paid off the mortgage." "When I get a promotion." "When I reach the age of retirement, then I shall live happily ever after."

Sooner or later, we must realize there is no station in this life. The true joy of life

> *The true joy of life is enjoying the Lord.*

is enjoying the Lord and His people on our way. The station is Jesus and we have arrived. Relish the moment, love the day and praise Him for life now. *"This is the day the LORD has made; let us rejoice and be glad in it."*[7] It isn't the burdens of today that drive men mad. It is the regrets over yesterday and the fear of tomorrow. Regret and fear are twin thieves who rob us of today. So, stop pacing the aisles and counting the miles. Instead, climb more mountains, eat more ice cream, go barefoot more often, swim more rivers, watch more sunsets, laugh more and cry less. Life must be lived as we go along. Love Jesus! Serve Him! Embrace your family! Relish your friends! Enjoy life abundantly and chill out!

Helen Keller declared that, "Security is mostly a superstition. It does not exist in nature, nor do the children of men as a whole experience it. Avoiding danger is no safer in the long run than outright exposure. Life is either a daring adventure or nothing."

Spiritual Compound Interest Principle # 3 --
Like the Fallen Tree, Bloom Where Your Lot in Life has Fallen

"Whether a tree falls to the south or to the north, in the place where it falls, there will it lie." [8]

We should greet each new day with this attitude in our hearts and these words on our lips: *"This is the day the LORD has made; let us rejoice and be glad in it."* [11] I have no promise of tomorrow. There is nothing that I can do about the fruit of yesterday's harvest, but I can begin to sow now for the future harvest. Praise God I am alive and I am going to invest in today and glorify God by enjoying Him in everything that I do.

Remember the song: "Sowing in the morning; sowing seeds of kindness; sowing in the noontime and the dewy evening?" If you keep sowing in all seasons and at all times, either you or future generations, will come rejoicing, bringing in the sheaves. In the confidence of this truth, be bold and resist the tendency to do nothing for fear of the unknown.

> *There is nothing that I can do about the fruit of yesterday's harvest!*

In St. Paul's Cathedral in London, there is a tablet in honor of Samuel A. Barnett, who preached to the rebellious, sinful people of East London for a half-century....a very difficult mission field! The tablet portrays an engraved figure of the sower, with these words: "Fear not to sow on account of the birds." You see, Barnett learned that sowing with this kind of people is NOT "just for the birds." Even hard, calloused people can be led to the Lord.

In fact, this particular parable was used to reach John Bunyan and lead him to Christ. That blasphemous tinker of Bedford was known as the most godless man in his village and was regarded as so hardhearted and committed to godlessness that no Christian had any hope for him at all. But Bunyan heard this story of the sower and these very words seized upon his heart. And he said to himself, "Even the devil knows that if a man believes the word he'll be saved."

Bunyan saw this Word sown in a person. A doctor who was a dissolute man, given to drink and gambling, soon had lost all he had. His gambling had made him destitute; his drinking had made him a drunk! But, there at the bottom of his life, despairing of everything, a book with gospel seeds fell into his hands. In his desperation he read it, and was guided by it to faith in Christ. The village was Bedford. The man John Gifford, the very man whom John Bunyan would later call "Holy Mister Gifford," and to whose doctrine and preaching John Bunyan would later owe his soul. It is this man--this former wastrel and drunk--who is immortalized as

"Evangelist" in Bunyan's *Pilgrim's Progress*.

As a result of the seed sown by these two men, Bunyan received it, wrapped faith around it, and was saved. He became the author of *Pilgrim's Progress* and a tremendous testimony for God in his age. Like a potter working with hard clay, if we let Him, God can break us even when we are hardhearted, and make us soft and pliable again....receptive to His leading.

Spiritual Compound Interest Principle # 4 -- Be Courageously Trusting in God's Sovereignty in the Face of Life's Mystery

"As you do not know the path of the wind, or how the body is formed in a mother's womb, so you cannot understand the work of God, the Maker of all things." [10]

In verse 5 we are admonished to not let baffling events stop us. Do not get bogged down by what you don't understand. Have you come to realize that you and I do not understand 99.999% of all there is to know? How dare we get bogged down by the mysterious and baffling things that we do not know. This means no more remorseful "if only." If only I had better parents. If only I had not grown up in this community. If only I had an opportunity to get a degree. If only I had married the right person. If only I had the right job. Respond to the opportunities that God gives you.

> *We are where we are because we have made the choices we've made.*

Be courageously trusting the living God. In those places and events when you cannot trace His hand, trust His heart.

There's a principle that I would like to bring out on this topic. We are where we are because we have made the choices we've made. If we want something we've never had, we need to start sowing seeds we've never sown. For many years of my life, I did not play golf for one reason or another. When I realized that golf had become a huge part of the life of my son, Thomas, I decided to sow seeds of golf in my life. I began to watch golf programming. I took lessons regularly. I also played several times a week; not just to play golf, but to maximize the time with my son. We know God is in charge of all our affairs, but He holds us responsible to work with the seeds we have. Now today, I am the greatest golfer alive.

Spiritual Compound Interest Principle # 5 -- Rest confidently in the promises of God to eventually bless and make our lives productive

"Sow your seed in the morning, and at evening let not your hands be idle, for you do not know which will succeed, whether this or that, or whether both will do equally well." [11]

Far too many settle for the "much less" of God's promised "much more". One person said, "I've lived my whole life by accident." Someone else said, "I'm a box of parts and nothing fits together. I feel like my life is a movie that is almost over and I haven't even bought the popcorn yet."

Mark Twain said, "Twenty years from now you will be more disappointed by the things that you didn't do than by the ones you did do. So throw off the bowlines. Sail away from the safe harbor. Catch the trade winds in your sails. Explore. Dream. Discover."

We should resolve to sow more good seed than we have ever sown before.

We should resolve to sow more good seed than we have ever sown before, to distribute more truth than ever before, to invest in more lives than ever before, to avail ourselves of every opportunity to sow seed: to sow seeds of the printed and spoken word; seeds of kindness, seeds of life-giving words and of life-imparting persons.

A believer by the name of George Smith was commissioned by the Moravians to go to the mission field in Africa. He was only there for a brief period of time when he was driven out of the country. He had only a single convert, a woman who was very destitute and un-influential in that community. After he had been driven from the country, he died a few months later, believing even on his deathbed that his life and labors had been in vain. All he had to show for all his years of preparation and effort in Africa was one single, undistinguished woman. A few years later missionaries were sent back into this area of Africa. They stumbled upon the area where this man, George Smith, had witnessed and worked. They were introduced to the lady that Smith had won to Christ. This lady began to unfold the story for these missionaries. She said after he was driven out she shared her testimony with others and there was a convert. This convert witnessed and won someone to Christ. Before long a church was established. Upon further investigation, they discovered that as a result of George Smith's witnessing and winning that one person to Christ, more than 13,000 had been converted!

Cast your bread upon the waters!

Spiritual Compound Interest Principle # 6—The Bad "Seeding" Law of the Compound Harvest Principle is Always in Force

We would be less than honest if we did not emphasize the negative side of the principle we have been studying: "We reap the same in kind as we sow and we reap far more than we sow!" The lyrics of a 1974 song released by Harry Chapin

What You Seed is What You Get!

on his "Verities and Balderdash" record album entitled "Cat's In The Cradle" illustrate so powerfully the negative side of this law of the harvest.

Cat's In The Cradle

A child arrived just the other day
He came to the world in the usual way
But there were planes to catch, and bills to pay
He learned to walk while I was away, and he was talkin'
'fore I knew it, and as he grew,
he says I'm gonna be like you,
Dad, you know I'm gonna be like you.

And the cat's in the cradle, and the silver spoon
Little boy blue and the man on the moon.
When you comin' home, Dad, I don't know when
But we'll get together then
You know we'll have a good time then.

My son turned ten just the other day, he said
Thanks for the ball, Dad, come on let's play
Can you teach me to throw, I said not today
I got a lot to do, he said that's okay
And he, he walked away but his smile never dimmed,
and said I'm gonna be like him, yeah
You know I'm gonna be like him.

Well he came from college just the other day
So much like a man I just had to say
Son I'm proud of you, can you sit for a while
He shook his head, and said, with a smile
What I'd really like, Dad, is to borrow the car keys

See ya later, can I have them please
And the cat's in the cradle, and the silver spoon
Little boy blue and the man on the moon.
When you comin' home, son, I don't know when
But we'll get together then, Dad,
You know we'll have a good time then.

I've long since retired, my son's moved away
I called him up just the other day
I said, I'd like to see you, if you don't mind, he said
I'd love to, Dad, if I could find the time
You see my new job's a hassle and the kids with the flu
But it's been sure nice talkin' to you, Dad
It's been sure nice talkin' to you
And as I hung up the phone it occurred to me
He'd grown up just like me
My boy was just like me!

Small was the thing I bought; small was the thing at best; small was the debt I thought, but O, God -- the interest!

Sow a thought, reap an act;
Sow an act, reap a habit;
Sow a habit, reap a character;
Sow a character, reap a destiny.
Sow a destiny and reap a legacy to be left for all those who come behind you.

We see a pattern emerge from this word progression. We can now further explain the parable of the sower and the seeds. The seeds we sow today become tomorrow's destiny. Our destiny is determined by what we put in the ground. Good seed into good soil produces 30, 60, or 100 fold return.

What You Seed is What You Get!

> 30 fold = 3,000% return
> 60 fold = 6,000% return
> 100 fold = 10,000% return

We know that some of our seed spills into bad soil, or the enemy takes some of the seed, but if that good seed is placed into good soil then the least we can expect to receive is 3,000% return. It could be 10,000%, but the minimum is 3,000% on good seed into good soil. This is why we continually sow good seed into good soil. It is time to start planting good seed into good soil. Only then can we expect the harvest for which we have believed.

Chapter Three:
Maintaining our Seed Planters...
or Learning to Manage our Mouths

Seeds are amazing things! They are a living pattern, a genetically coded structure, a word-by-word set of instructions that under the right circumstances will reproduce its parent, with unity in diversity.

Our bodies began with two half-seeds -- one called an egg and the other a sperm -- the seed of the man and the seed of the woman. There is little doubt as to why God said that we are fearfully and wonderfully made. Just think of what a miracle you really are. Hundreds of thousands of sperm racing towards that one egg and yours won! Always remember that you have been a winner from your conception. You started out that way, so end that way. From this whole seed developed a vast collection of cells, some one hundred trillion in number, each of them containing twenty-three pairs of chromosomes, that make you--you! Winding through each pair of chromosomes, is the double spiral of the DNA molecule, the genetic blueprint for life. The DNA, abbreviation for deoxyribonucleic acid, is the word system of instructions built within every living cell.

Every DNA is comprised of approximately 3.3 billion individual pieces, each a complimentary pair, with

Always remember that you have been a winner from your conception.

each pair composed of four bases. The DNA in any cell of your one hundred trillion is sufficient, if we could "read" and obey all the instructions, to reconstruct your whole body just as it is. The information stored in one cell of your body is enough to fill a book with 600,000 pages. If the DNA in one of your cells were strung out in a straight line, it would stretch from the earth to the sun and back four hundred times!

Puritan Thomas Manton wrote, "Whatever we do in this life is seed; as we sow, so we reap."

You will recall from the previous chapter that we defined a good or bad seed as follows: A good seed is a word, a pattern, a vision, a picture or an idea for changing creation to conform to God's design. A bad seed is a word, a pattern, a vision, a picture, an idea for changing creation to continued rebellion against God's design.

It's been aptly stated, "We are farmers, you and I, even if we never touch a shovel or pitchfork, or sit in the sloping rugged seat of a tractor, or pray that the frost will not come, not now anyway, not now; even if we don't know what wheat, barley, or rye looks like, even if we don't get up at 3:30 in the morning to pull on muddy boots. Wherever we work, we are farmers: we plant seeds every day. Our thoughts are seeds, our words are seeds, and our actions are seeds. Preparing, planting, and nurturing these seeds must become a precise and inspirational art. We must take great care to plant seeds worthy of the abundant future we desire.

If whatever we do in this life is seed, and if words are seeds, then our mouths are the seed

> *Every word-seed has the potential for either blessing or cursing.*

planters. This makes the use of our tongues of the utmost importance because the most frequently planted seeds are our words. Every word-seed has the potential for either blessings or curses. Solomon said, *"The tongue has the power of life and death, and those who love it will eat its fruit."* [1] Your words are packed with spiritual power and can have lasting beneficial or devastating effects on those to whom they are directed. In addition, once released, blessings and curses continue through time until their power is revoked or annulled.

"There are some things that almost everyone possesses, everyone uses, and often abuses. They are near to the heart, touch the heart, melt, break and heal the heart. They are fleeting things; they come and go in an instant, but they last forever. Though they cost nothing they are treasures of immense value. They are not cheap but too often very costly. They can destroy lives or build fortunes. They are used every day, almost every minute of every day, but are too often wasted. By them we are known. With them we either heal or harm, help or hurt, bless or curse. Without them life would be oh so lonely." – What are they? They are words!

The Oxford English Dictionary contains around 60,000 words in the English language. The biggest dictionary has more than 400,000 entries. According to the American Heritage Dictionary, there are 884,647 known English words.

Author Chris Simpson says, "A dictionary is a marvelous thing but useless in putting words together. Stringing these words together you can build fortunes, sway nations, win followers, cheat investors, ruin lives and destroy reputations. The pen is mightier than the sword because the pen writes words. Words mean things, do things, change things, influence things, and make things happen. Words are alive. Once uttered they can never be taken back."

> *The pen is mightier than the sword because the pen writes words.*

In a lifetime of 75 years, if we average 3500 words per day for 70 of those years, we would have to give an account to the Lord for 89,425,000 words in a lifetime!

Our words betray us. Like fingerprints left at the scene of the crime or footprints in the sand, they follow us, they point back to us.

In light of this, it becomes obvious that the key to being a successful life-farmer is learning to maintain our "seed-planters," which being interpreted means learning to "manage our mouths" so that we plant blessings and not curses.

Mouth-management is the Measure of Maturity

"We all stumble in many ways. If anyone is never at fault in what he says, he is a perfect man, able to keep his whole body in check." [2]

The Bible has much to say about the potential of the

tongue or the words that we sow. It refers to a wicked tongue, a lying tongue, a perverse tongue, a bitter tongue, a flattering tongue, a gossiping, slandering tongue, a murmuring, complaining, cursing tongue, a boasting, blaspheming tongue, a tale-bearing tongue, etc.. Most problems in life involve the tongue. There's no easier way to sin than via the tongue. There's nothing more dangerous than a tongue that's loose on both ends and continually flapping! These persons could talk their head off and never miss it. They make you think of a river -- small at the head and big at the mouth!

A Greek philosopher asked his servant to provide the best dish possible. The servant prepared a dish of tongue, saying, "It is the best of all dishes because with it we may bless and communicate happiness, dispel sorrow, remove despair, cheer the faint-hearted, inspire the discouraged, and say a hundred other things to uplift mankind." Later the philosopher asked his servant to provide the worst dish of which he could think. A dish of tongue appeared on the table. The servant said, "It is the worst because with it we may curse and break human hearts, destroy reputations, promote discord and strife, set families and communities and nations at war with each other."

These words from an anonymous author underscore the power of spoken words:

A careless word may kindle strife;
A cruel word may wreck a life;
A bitter word may hate instill;
A brutal word may often kill.
But-
A gracious word will smooth the way;
A joyous word will light the day;

A timely word will lessen stress;
A lovely word will heal and bless.

Pay very close attention to the truth set forth in the following proverbs:

"if you have been trapped by what you said, ensnared by the words of your mouth," [3]

"An evil man is trapped by his sinful talk, but a righteous man escapes trouble. From the fruit of his lips a man is filled with good things as surely as the work of his hands rewards him." [7][4]

"Reckless words pierce like a sword, but the tongue of the wise brings healing." [5]

"Truthful lips endure forever, but a lying tongue lasts only a moment. " [6]

"The tongue that brings healing is a tree of life, but a deceitful tongue crushes the spirit." [7]

"The tongue has the power of life and death, and those who love it will eat its fruit. " [8]

"He who guards his mouth and his tongue keeps himself from calamity." [9]

> *He who has a sharp tongue usually cuts his own throat.*

According to the book of James, the tongue has the power to direct, destroy or delight.

No wonder God put our tongues in a cage behind our teeth, walled in by our mouths! Someone rightly said "The

58

tongue is in a wet place and can slip easily." Another person said that "A slip of the lip can get you hung by the tongue." He who has a sharp tongue usually cuts his own throat.

The Curse that the Tongue Sows Has the Pattern for Multiplying Frustration

"With the tongue we praise our Lord and Father, and with it we curse men, who have been made in God's likeness. Out of the same mouth come praise and cursing. My brothers, this should not be. Can both fresh water and salt water flow from the same spring? My brothers, can a fig tree bear olives, or a grapevine bear figs? Neither can a salt spring produce fresh water. " [10]

The words bless or blessings occur around 410 times in the Bible. The word curse occurs around 230 times. We here in the West readily accept the idea of blessings but tend to relegate curses to ancient times or to backward, ignorant parts of the world today.

The word translated blessing in James 3:9, is "eulegeo" which means to "speak well of." The English word eulogy is derived from this Greek word. We now understand what the funeral eulogies were designed for. The Greek word translated curse is "kataraomai," (kat-ar-ah'-om-ahee). It's made up of two words -- kata = down, and araomai = pray -- to pray down negative results. Curses are words which are spoken against another person or one's self with intent to harm. The words in themselves have no authority to hurt; it is the spiritual power behind the words that enables the terms of the curse to be fulfilled.

Cursing in the Bible isn't the use of swear words or dirty

words. Neither is blessing just a nice way of wishing health and wealth for someone. Cursing and blessing are a power concept meant to release good or evil toward their object. To the Hebrew mind, a word was not just a

> *Cursing and blessing are a powerful concept meant to release good or evil toward their object.*

mere sound on the lips, but an agent sent forth. Thus the spoken curse was an active agent sent forth with the design to do harm and bring hurt.

Blessings and curses are formal pronouncements by someone in authority; in the case of blessing, bestowing God's positive empowerment. Not only are they formal proclamations, but they are understood as words of power; the words bring the desired result to fruition. Balak, the Moabite king, says to Balaam: *"...For I know that those you bless are blessed, and those you curse are cursed."* [11]

To sum up what we have been saying: Curses are words that set in motion legal authority to enforce the terms stated. Curses bring frustration, fruitlessness, failure, and futility to a people. Blessings are words of acceptance, affection, appreciation, approval and attention that encourage, enrich and motivate us to become majestic trees of righteousness that finish life well.

Spoken Curses Create Frustration, Disorder and Evil Works

A bitter fountain and a barren fruit-tree

"Can both fresh water and salt water flow from the same

spring? My brothers, can a fig tree bear olives, or a grapevine bear figs? Neither can a salt spring produce fresh water. " 12

Word curses produce "frustration" -- patterns of failure, fruitlessness, and defeat that reappear over and over in areas such as business, careers, relationships, finances, or health.

Curses produce disorder and lack of peace. Peace comes from order and order from being submitted to the right government. Disorder comes from rebellion against authority. Our English word "rebellion" is made up of two words, re = again, and bellum = war, i.e. to war again.

"For rebellion is like the sin of divination, and arrogance like the evil of idolatry. Because you have rejected the word of the LORD, he has rejected you as king."13

One of the most life-impacting, success-stopping, and bondage-producing factors in life centers on the seed of word curses sown into our lives by significant others or by our own tongues.

Parents, failing to manage their mouths sow seed into their children's hearts that has a devastating effect. Some of those word curses are: "You are useless. You'll never be any good. You're just like your mother. Big boys don't cry. You'll never get married. Who would want to live with you? You're ugly. You'll never get a job. Never trust men, they'll only get you into trouble. You're really bad. You'll probably wind up in prison. You'll never change. Be on the watch for this physical problem, it's in the family and you'll most likely have it."

Children rarely know how to deal with cruel words constructively.

What You Seed is What You Get!

Unfortunately, children rarely know how to handle the sort of situation when cruel words are spoken against them. The arrows usually find their target. Inside, the child (and often the adult) will make an inner vow. This is a form of self-curse through which we determine not to let these things happen again, whatever it may cost us.

Negative, unscriptural self-talk takes on the form of word curses and inner vows against ourselves. This sets us in a lifestyle or an attitude that is contrary to God's plan and purpose. Our potential for success in life is limited and we invite the enemy to control us.

Read carefully some of the following inner vows and word curses that have brought frustration, failure and faith loss in people's lives.

"I'll never forgive myself. I'm ugly, fat, useless, a nuisance, etc." These types of confessions are inner vows that are a direct response to believing that what others have said against them must be true.

Karen Carpenter was part of a duo called "The Carpenters." They had many hit records that are still played often on some of the "oldie" stations. Karen died unexpectedly of heart failure at age 32 brought on by years of self abuse from the eating disorder Anorexia Nervosa. But what brought on Karen's fatal obsession with weight control? USA TODAY reported that it all started when a reviewer once called her "Richard's chubby sister."

"I'll never speak to, associate with.....again. It'll be a cold day in you know where before I have anything to do with them." These words are inner vows which are a direct response to damage caused by someone.

"It's not safe to look attractive. If I make myself look attractive I may get rejected or abused again." Deliberately getting overweight or anorexic are typical responses to hide one's sexuality. These are common responses to this type of negative self-programming. Caution: words program your mind.

> *Negative self-talk is verbal abuse.*

"I want to die; I'm better off dead. I'll probably die with the same disease that killed my Mom or Dad and four other generations in the family."

"Sex is dirty" was the response of a child who asked her parents questions about the facts of life. Her response to her parents' embarrassment was to conclude that sex must be very dirty. Sexual problems in marriage may be attributed to this inner vow.

Negative self-talk is verbal abuse. Someone estimated that 85% of the conversation we experience every day is us talking to ourselves. The average person's self-talk is 90% negative! We have met the enemy and he is us when we allow our own tongues to beat us up and put us down by verbal abuse.

If most of us talked to other people the way we talk to ourselves, we would be at best friendless and at worst beaten about the head and shoulders and broke from lawsuits of slander and character assassination!

Husbands, failing to manage their mouths, sow seed into their wife's heart. Said by husbands to wives -- "Why can't you cook like my mother? You are pathetic. You dress like a clown. When I see you in bed I feel like sleeping in the spare room. Why can't you be like John's wife?"

What You Seed is What You Get!

Wives, failing to manage their mouths, sow seed into their husband's heart. Said by wives to husbands -- "I wish I'd married a real man. All you're interested in is sex (to a man who was heart-broken by his wife's total lack of interest in him as a person). It's a pity the children haven't got someone they can look up to. You're just like your father - useless. No wonder you can't get a job. I wouldn't employ you for anything."

Sometimes out of ignorance or insensitivity we wind up like the following husband and wife who were getting ready for bed. When the wife, standing in front of a full-length mirror taking a hard look at herself says, "You know, dear, I look in the mirror, and I see an old woman. My face is all wrinkled, my hair is grey, my shoulders are hunched over. I've got fat legs, and my arms are all flabby." She turns to her husband and says, "Tell me something positive to make me feel better about myself."

He studies hard for a moment thinking about it and then says in a soft, thoughtful voice, "Well, at least you've got great eyesight."

It is time to stop the negative effects of word-curses spoken over you or by you. The following is a prayer by Liberty Savard that expresses the need you have to be free from the bad seed sown into your heart. Get before the Lord and pray it in sincerity and faith.

Put a stop to the power of negative word-curses.

"Lord, I loose the influence and the effects of all word curses (known or unknown) spoken about me, to me, and by me. Forgive me for word curses I have spoken upon myself. I bind myself to the truth of the Word which tells me I can do all things through Jesus Christ, who strengthens me. I bind myself to the truth of the Word that Jesus has given me His peace, which the world cannot take away. I bind myself to the truth of the Word that all things work together for my good. I am not limited by anyone else's opinions of my life and my abilities unless I choose to come into wrong agreement with such limitations. I loose every wrong agreement I've ever believed and entered into regarding negative words spoken to me or about me. I bind myself to the truth of the Word that I am a new creature in Christ. Old things have passed away. All things are new and waiting for me to receive them. In Jesus' name, Amen."

Mouth-management requires that we Focus on Sowing Good Seed and not on Canceling Bad Seed Sown by Others or Ourselves

We are not responsible to be constantly trying to free ourselves from all unknown word curses. Attempting to do this will cause us to become paranoid and live controlled by the fear that others are secretly trying to do us in.

The truth is, blessings and cursings are an every day occurrence. Yet, the disciples didn't go about removing curses, but they did impart blessings.

Keep your word-planter full of good-seeds so that you sow in peace
"Peacemakers who sow in peace raise a harvest of righteousness." 14

That goes for all of you. No exceptions. No retaliation. No sharp-tongued sarcasm. Instead, bless. That's your job. To bless. You'll be a blessing and also get a blessing.

It is by speaking blessings and not curses that we plant the Word-Seeds of Identity and Destiny

When Peter says that blessing those who insult us is our divine calling, and that this calling is a condition of inheriting our future blessing, he's not saying that we earn our future blessing with meritorious works. He is saying you must truly be born again; you must put your hope and your faith so genuinely in that blessing (of being a partaker of the divine nature via the new birth) that the quality of that gracious blessing is absorbed from the future into the present and shows in your life by blessing others.

In the Bible, the Hebrews named their children with names that were a small sentence. For example, Daniel means "God is my Judge," or "God is my Deliverer." Elijah means "Jehovah is God." Jonathan means "God's Gracious Gift." Joshua means "The Lord is Salvation." In so naming their children, the Hebrew parents desired God to give powerful impartations to who their children were and what their destiny was to be.

> *Blessings and cursings are part of everyone's everyday experience.*

We are called to bless the nations – *"The Scripture foresaw that God would justify the Gentiles by faith, and announced the gospel in advance to Abraham: "All nations will be blessed through you. So those who have faith are blessed along with Abraham, the man of faith."* [15] *"He redeemed us in order that the blessing given to Abraham might come to the Gentiles through Christ Jesus, so that by faith we might receive the promise of the Spirit."* [16]

God sent His Son to Bless us – " *When God raised up his servant, he sent him first to you to bless you by turning each of you from your wicked ways"* [17]

"Bless those who persecute you; bless and do not curse." [18]

Speaking blessing is an impartation of God's message of identity and destiny. In other words, who God says you are. When we talk about identity we are talking about who am I. When we talk about destiny we are talking about where am I going and what is my purpose on the earth.

There are two ultimate sources for answers to the questions - Who am I and where am I going? One is God and one is the Enemy.

For instance, in parenting, the parents can be the agents of God to impart the child's God-given identity or destiny (who one really is and where one is going), or they can be the Enemy's agent to impart a false identity or destiny. God's message and the Enemy's message were, of course, total opposites. The Enemy would want to impart to a person's

> *Speaking a blessing imparts God's message of identity and destiny.*

heart: "You are nothing. You are nobody. You are born the wrong sex. You are not wanted, not loved, just a product of someone's lust. You don't have what it takes to succeed. You are stupid. You are unspiritual. You are ugly." These words foster ruin in a person's life.

God's message is just the opposite: "I love you. You are precious. You are special. You are supposed to be here. You have a purpose. You have a destiny. No one else can fulfill your call and destiny." You are the only one that can accomplish what

God has put you on the earth to do. No one else can be a father to your children or a husband to your wife. No one else can be a daughter to your parents. No one else can accomplish what you have been sent here to accomplish.

Cursing is an impartation that isn't of God. Imparting negativity into a person's life can lead to bondage. The curse usually comes through a human agency, often times through parents who sometimes give just the opposite message from what God wants given. Their words touch the child on the inside and create an image and the emotions and feelings that go along with it.

Craig Hill tells of a man who shared a story with him about how that when he was in first grade, just a little boy 6 years old, his father apparently wanted to motivate him to try harder in school. His father was a wealthy businessman. He took him for a ride in a brand new Cadillac one day and said to his son, "Enjoy the ride son because you will never have one of these, because you are stupid." Now if you look at whose message that was - that wasn't God's message being imparted to that little boy. That was the Enemy''s message being imparted - "You are stupid. You won't amount to anything." And that message hit the inside of that little boy's heart and stuck there and he spent a lifetime fighting against those words trying to make something of himself. But a feeling got imparted deep on the inside that was a cursing of identity, not a blessing of identity - a message that came from the Enemy that wounded something deep on the inside. Thirty-five or forty years later that man was still fighting to try to undo the message that his father imparted to him. He became a successful business man himself, owned many Cadillacs, and drove them to his father's house trying to get his father to eat those words. But his father never did. The man almost lost his wife and his children in an attempt to overcome the deep wounding that had come from that curse uttered by his father in ignorance. The father didn't know that he made himself an agent of the Enemy that day to impart something that didn't come from God.

Put your word-seeds to the test before you sow them

What is their source? Will the words that I am about to speak reflect the wisdom that is from above or the corruptness from below?

"Such 'wisdom' does not come down from heaven but is earthly, unspiritual, of the devil. For where you have envy and selfish ambition, there you find disorder and every evil practice. But the wisdom that comes from heaven is first of all pure; then peace-loving, considerate, submissive, full of mercy and good fruit, impartial and sincere." [19]

> But the wisdom from above is first pure, then peaceable, gentle, open to reason, full of mercy and good fruits, impartial and sincere.

Are the words I am considering speaking true but it's not the time to sow them? There is a time to speak the truth in love and then there are times when the most loving and powerfully impacting thing we can do is be silent.

Is what I say consistent with what I do? In other words, am I talking a future harvest of wheat while I'm sowing wild oats?

Dr. Lynn Reddick, in writing of the power of the spoken word says, "Tongue power is released through spoken words that either bless or curse, build up or degrade. Having God's divine nature within enables us to be ambassadors of encouragement to other people. As we establish the blessing habit, we can see the positive effect upon people (including ourselves) in 30 days or less.

> *Am I talking a future harvest of wheat while I'm sowing wild oats?*

Take the challenge and be filled with the Spirit in a fresh way and begin to establish the blessing habit by a thirty day commitment to bless and curse not! Speak blessings over mates, children, grandchildren, fellow believers, upline, downline, and over yourself!

Each morning and evening speak these things aloud over yourself and your family:

- I am a child of God.
- I am being sanctified.
- I am uniquely privileged.
- I am highly favored.
- I am immeasurably loved.
- I am eternally secure.
- God's power keeps me.
- God's might upholds me.
- God's wisdom teaches me.
- The eyes of God watch over me.
- The ears of God hear me.
- The word of God speaks to me.
- The hand of God supplies me.
- The way of God is before me.
- The shield of God shelters me.
- I am who He says I am.
- I can do what He says I can do.
- I can have what He says I can have.

Blessing the Lord

"I will extol the LORD at all times; his praise will always be on my lips." [20]

How can you bless God? Obviously you can't add to His happiness, increase His greatness, bolster His glory, or enlarge His goodness. We bless the Lord by daily thinking well of Him, speaking well of Him and worshipping and praising Him. We do it with all of our being. Our minds are to know God, our wills choose Him, our hearts go after Him, our confidence leans on Him, our love delights in Him, our tongues praise Him, our knees bow to Him and our hands clap for joy of Him.

Blessings for Families

"because of your father's God, who helps you, because of the Almighty, who blesses you with blessings of the heavens above, blessings of the deep that lies below, blessings of the breast and womb." [21]

By the Almighty God, El Shaddai, the one who pours forth Himself in blessings, I bless you with the blessings of heaven above. May you know that the Father's countenance is upon you, and may He give you peace. May the LORD bless you and keep you and make His face shine upon you, and be gracious to you.

May you prosper and be in health because your soul prospers.

May you know daily that who God says you are, you are; that what He says you have, you have; that what He says you can do in order to fulfill your destiny, you can do.

May you walk in the dignity, authority, integrity, vitality, joy, and destiny of your birthright. May you be blessed with a long and fruitful life that plants good seeds that will provide a harvest for generations to come.

Blessings for Yourself

I am a blessed and highly favored believer in the Lord Jesus Christ. I have trusted in Him as Personal Savior and do now confess Him to be my Sovereign Lord. I am in Him, and He is in me in the Person of the Holy Spirit whom Jesus personally sent to re-create His likeness in me and re-present His life through me.

I am blessed in that the enemy has no place in me or power over me because I am in Christ, and he has no place in Him. I am in Him who has all things under His feet, and nothing under His feet is over my head.

I am blessed in knowing that who God says Jesus is, He is; what God says I am, I am. What He says I have, I have. What He says I can do, I can do all things through Christ who is my strength.

Because I am blessed and highly favored of the Lord, I will talk from a position of being the head and not the tail, of being blessed and not cursed, of having access to abundance and not shortages, of being filled with faith and not fear, worship and not worry, of being a grateful child of God and not a griping one!

> *May you be blessed with a long, fruitful life, planting good seeds.*

I will confess such blessings, whether I feel like it or not. I reject and renounce any thought or feeling contrary to the Word of God and receive and declare to be true all that comes from the Word of God.

Because I am blessed with all spiritual blessings in Christ, I renounce all bondage in my mind and body and claim the Holy Spirit's fresh filling and anointing as I make these confessions in accordance with the Word and Spirit of God. I declare by faith that I overcome the Accuser by the blood of the Lamb, by the words of this confession, and declare my commitment to the death if necessary. Whatever God has said, I may boldly say ... so I speak what He speaks ... in Jesus' Name, Amen!

Blessings Upon a Couple

I speak blessings upon you _____ and _____ and ask the Lord to go on prospering and keeping you both in health, because you constantly realize that except the Lord build the house, those who build labor in vain.

May the Lord go on leading you into such situations as will bless you and continue to develop your character as you walk together. May He go on giving you enough tears to keep you tender, enough hurts to keep you compassionate, enough failure to keep your hands clenched tightly in His, and your knees bent constantly in prayer. May He give you enough success to make sure that you always having sufficiency in all things may abound to every good work.

May the light of friendship guide your paths together. May the halls of your home ring with holy laughter. May your children and future grandchildren, rise up to consider themselves highly privileged to have had such parents as you two.

May the joy of living with and for one another for these many years go on evoking a smile from your lips, and a twinkle from your eye, and a prayer of gratitude from your hearts. May our Lord continue to bless you with a long and fruitful life together, and when life is done, may you be found then as now, hand in hand, still thanking God for each other. May you continue to serve Him happily and faithfully -- together -- until you return to glory, or until at last one shall lay the other into His arms. And all this through Jesus Christ our Lord.

Bless and curse not!

Chapter Four:
Wait Training
A Strategic Discipline
for "Seeding" to Success

A cartoon in the newspaper showed a man ready to leap from the ledge of a high-rise apartment building with a suicide note in his hand but with a parachute strapped to his back. His wife, leaning out of the window, says to him, "Just can't make a commitment to anything can you, Larry?"

This cartoon, though funny, nevertheless makes a very telling statement about modern society. The time-honored character traits of faithfulness, commitment, and perseverance have been jettisoned upon the rolling rocks of relativism – no absolutes, nothing is nailed-down or true, everything is in flux. With this predominating view of reality, one shouldn't be surprised that, like Larry in the cartoon, hardly any are willing to commit or be faithful to anyone or anything these days. Without a commitment to persevere until the harvest comes, success in life miscarries before fruition.

Our text reveals that the church in Galatia was comprised of a little company of Christian men and women who had been given the assignment of cultivating a patch of tough, rough, and most unpromising spiritual ground. The moral atmosphere surrounding them was stifling and heavy with the enemy's presence. The soil, or human hearts, that they had to work with was hard and unclean. It was interpenetrated with roots of ancient customs, pagan religions and traditions, and powerful enemy strongholds. Some of the little company of life-farmers took the path of least resistance and began to act selfishly and exclusively; they were fencing off their own lives, and devoting themselves solely to the culture of their own souls. They were beginning to "look every man on his own things," and not upon "the things of others." All this made it terribly hard for the earnest and zealous workers who were seeking in the worldwide field to turn the desert into a garden and to make the wilderness rejoice and blossom as the rose. They had planted good seeds, but now they were in "Wait Training." This is the season between the sowing and the reaping. Without proper "wait" training, quitting seems the easiest and most logical choice as we begin to grow weary in well-doing.

Without a commitment to persevere until the harvest comes, success in life miscarries before fruition.

As Americans, we are not into waiting on anything. Few, if any of us, respond well to making a phone call and being put on hold before we have a chance to say a word, or waiting for an hour before we finally get to speak to a real live person instead of recordings. Americans don't like to wait. We are irritated by slow moving lines, by waiting to be seated at the restaurant; or even waiting to meet a friend who is always late.

Ours is a world of going, doing, and having instantly, not one of active waiting. We want quick answers, instant access, and immediate solutions to our problems.

The life-farmers that the Apostle Paul wrote to in Galatia had no doubt often stopped in the field of their assignment with tired and aching limbs, and with depressed, discouraged, and weary hearts, and sent a tired cry to the bending heavens, "Lord how long? How long?" It is to men and women like these, contending valiantly against overwhelming odds, that the Lord sends this heartening and triumphant, faith-building word, *"Let us not become weary in doing good, for at the proper time we will reap a harvest if we do not give up."* [1]

> *Without proper wait training, quitting seems the most logical choice.*

"Wait" Training Requires Having a Right Perspective on Time and the Harvest

We Must Patiently Cooperate with the Process that Leads to the Harvest

"Be patient, then, brothers, until the Lord's coming. See how the farmer waits for the land to yield its valuable crop and how patient he is for the autumn and spring rains. You too, be patient and stand firm, because the Lord's coming is near. Don't grumble against each other, brothers, or you will be judged. The Judge is standing at the door!" [2]

There are two different words in the Greek for patience. The first word translated patience is "makrothumeo." It means to be long-fused with people, so that one does not yield to the passion of retaliatory anger. The idea is to stick with people even though they test your limits! [3]

The second word translated patience is "hupomone" (hoop-om-on-ay). It carries the meaning endurance, constancy, and patient continuance, i.e., waiting. Thayer's Greek Lexicon defines the word as "a patient, steadfast waiting for, constancy, endurance. It is characteristic of a man who is not swerved from his deliberate purpose and his loyalty to faith and piety by even the greatest trials and suffering." [3]

Once we combine the ideas behind these two Greek words, we begin to understand our one

Our work is like farming, we often work in the dark!

English word, patience. We begin to understand that people problems and circumstancial problems require us to stay under the pressure and wait on God to change both us and the problems. Even if the problems never change or the persons involved leave us, we are made better by our responding in grace rather than reacting by griping and as a result we have a greater impact upon others and our circumstances than they have on us! If we continually attempt to avoid or run from every difficulty in relationships or from every hardship, pressure, pain and problem in life, we will find that our reaping leaves us far short of a successful harvest.

A basic life principle for successful life-farming is a reminder that: "If our work is like farming, we will often find ourselves working in the dark!"

A second basic life principle for successful life-farming is: "Don't assume the harvest is in hand just because the seed has been sown!

Since so much of our work is like farming, we must

always be mindful of being partners with mighty and mysterious forces. Jesus described this mysterious partnership this way: *"He also said, 'This is what the kingdom of God is like. A man scatters seed on the ground. Night and day, whether he sleeps or gets up, the seed sprouts and grows, though he does not know how. All by itself the soil produces grain — first the stalk, then the head, then the full kernel in the head. As soon as the grain is ripe, he puts the sickle to it, because the harvest has come.'"* 4

In the Far East the people plant a tree called the Chinese bamboo. During the first four years they water and fertilize the plant with seemingly little or no results. Then the fifth year they again apply water and fertilizer -- and in five weeks' time the tree has grown to ninety feet in height. Question -- Did the tree grow ninety feet in five weeks or in five years? In five years... because if they had stopped caring for it at anytime during the five years it would have died. Likewise life-farmers must not consider time wasted when they are cooperating with God's laws of the harvest.

As sons of God, we have invisible and tremendous allies -- the seed of the Word of God, the Spirit of God, the angels of God, the sons of God, the predestined plan of Father God, and the effectual prayer of the Son of God! If we are consistently and correctly aligning ourselves with all of the above, we are assured of success as defined by God – finding out how God made us to function and functioning consistently in His power to fulfill His purpose in our life.

A third basic life principle for successful life-farming is a reminder that: "We Must Avoid Shortcuts that Negate the Wait!"

The easiest way out is usually the quickest way down. Instant success does not exist. Sin is the great short-cut. The

What You Seed is What You Get!

Enemy offers us instant gratification with demonic "enhancement": You can be "spiritual"... You can be "wise and wealthy"... You can be "attractive"... You can have "fun"... You can "cope" NOW! As soon as we've been lured in, bad seed is sown, satisfaction becomes ever more elusive, and a bad harvest is on its way to maturity.

> *Sin is the greatest waster of time. Sin has immediate short-term benefits but an incredibly costly kick-back.*

God gives everlasting power to those who wait on Him to perform what He has promised. What we receive through faith will last forever. The Enemy gives temporary power to those who believe his lies. He becomes their "father" and they become his possession. One of the biggest challenges in life is foregoing immediate gratification for the ultimate eternal satisfaction.

Wait Training Requires Having a Right Perception of Trials and the Harvest

Trying times are no time to quit trying!

In the Scripture, three specific examples are given to encourage us not to quit during trying times. The farmer -- waits on the former and latter rains; the Prophets -- most sowed for another generation to reap; Job -- in spite of incredible tragedy and hardship, in the end received back double what the enemy had stolen from him! From these examples, God is saying our experiences are not unique and our problems are not unbearable.

> *Trying times are no time to quit trying!*

If Sir Winston Churchill had followed the example of Neville Chamberlain and many of his own advisors, he would have run away from Hitler's war machine which had overrun France in just 100 days. Today, the British might well be living under tyranny. Instead, Churchill said "Never give up! Never! Never! Never give up!" He went on to say, "Success in life is often nothing more than going from one failure to the next with undiminished enthusiasm."

The Harvest you Reap may not be Exactly what You Wanted, but it will be According to what You Expected!

Take heed how you perceive because it controls to a great extent what you receive! Be careful what you expect because you'll probably get it!

Trials that test my patience, insult my intelligence and humble my proud flesh are often the very trails that lead to success.

Charles Spurgeon tells of a young man who felt called of God to go to India as a missionary with the London Missionary Society. A man named Mr. Wilks was appointed to consider the young man's fitness for the position.

He wrote the man and told him to be at his office at 6 am. The man lived many miles away and had to leave in the wee hours of

> *Take heed how you perceive because it controls to a great extent what you receive!*

the morning to arrive promptly on time at 6 am. He was ushered into the visitor's waiting room and waited and waited until 10am. Finally he was told that Mr. Wilks would see him.

Without apology, Mr. Wilks began. "Well, young man, do you love the Lord Jesus Christ?"

"Yes sir, I do."

"Have you any education?"

"Yes sir, I do."

"Well, now I'll try you; can you spell cat?"

The young man looked confused. He halted between anger and submission, but in a moment replied, "C-A-T, cat!"

"Very good," said Mr. Wilks, "Now can you spell dog?"

He was stunned, and about ready to ask was this some sort of joke, but replied, "D-O-G, dog."

"Well, that's right; I see you will do well in spelling, and now for your math; how much is 2 multiplied by 2?"

The patient youth gave the right reply and then was dismissed.

Mr. Wilks gave his report to the missionary society: He said, "I whole-heartedly recommend this young man; his testimony and character I have duly examined. I tried his self-denial; he was up early in the morning; I tried his patience, keeping him waiting; I tried his humility and temper by insulting his intelligence. He will do just fine!"

What is the difference between a trial that seems senseless and keeps us waiting and waiting, and a trail that eventually leads on to the harvest? It is the position of the "I"! If we put ourselves in front of everything and everyone; if we put our dreams, our desires, our demands for immediate gratification first, then we will be forever in trials and never find the trail to successful life-farming. So be very careful what you expect because you very well may get it!

Wait Training Requires Having Resolute Patience in Order to Get the Treasure of the Harvest

The Lord Waits for Those Who Wait Upon Him in Order to be Gracious

"Yet the LORD longs to be gracious to you; he rises to show you compassion. For the LORD is a God of justice. Blessed are all who wait for him!" [5]

Lewis Smedes was on target when he wrote, "Waiting is our destiny as creatures who cannot by themselves bring about what they hope for. We wait in the darkness for a flame we cannot light. We wait for a happy ending we cannot write. We wait for a not yet that feels like a not ever." Long on ideas, short on time, Smedes finishes, "Waiting is the hardest work of hope."

Dutch Sheets summed up the typical American Christian's approach to life when he said, "We are into microwaving; God, on the other hand, is usually into marinating!" We are into "working" for the Lord, but not into "waiting" on the Lord. Our prayer is, "Lord, give me patience and give it to me now!"

> *We are into microwaving.*
> *God is usually into marinating!*

John Mason summed up the consequences of not waiting on the Lord: "Impatience is one big Get-A-Head-Ache!"

Successful Waiting Requires Strengthening Our Hearts to Avoid Rage and Retaliation

"You too, be patient and stand firm, because the Lord's coming is near." [6]

What does it mean to "wait upon the Lord?" It does not mean just sitting on my thumbs, doing nothing.

There are three Old Testament words used for waiting upon the Lord that give insight into the ways of waiting:

• *waits in silence (dumiyah), i.e., silently waiting with a quiet trust.* [7]

• *our soul waits for the Lord (chakah), i.e., longing for God's company.* [8]

• *wait for the Lord (qavah); who wait upon the Lord (qavah), i.e., eager expectation and oneness; a joining, a braiding together.* [9]

Putting all three of these Hebrew words together we get a clear picture of what it means to wait upon the Lord: Silently waiting with a strong, calm trust, longing for His presence and eagerly expecting Him. You know He will show up, so anticipate and then experience the oneness that results as your heart becomes entwined with His!

Successful Waiting on God Requires that I Shut my Mouth Rather than Grumble Against Others

"Don't grumble against each other, brothers, or you will be judged. The Judge is standing at the door!" [10]

Always remember that another man's blessing is never your loss. God has an abundance for everybody. To paraphrase the above passage, what James is saying to us is, "Don't compare your garden with someone else's." Failure to heed this admonishment leads to murmuring and complaining about the unfairness of life.

Puritan Jeremiah Burroughs: "When discontentment comes, it grows to murmuring, and you can go into no house almost, but there is murmuring when men are discontented, so that within a little while it breaks forth

Another man's blessing is never your loss!

into sedition or rebellion. Murmuring is but as the smoke of the fire: there is first smoke and smoldering before the flame breaks forth; and so before open rebellion in a kingdom there is first the smoke of murmuring, and then it breaks forth into open rebellion. But because it has the seeds of rebellion, it is accounted before the Lord to be rebellion."

Paul tells us to *"Do everything without complaining or arguing,"* [11]

In the wilderness, the children of Israel got themselves hung by their tongues by murmuring against God. The Apostle Paul writes that we are not to *"And do not grumble, as some of them did — and were killed by the destroying angel."* [12] Why is God so severe in His prohibitions against murmuring? Because murmuring, negativity, complaining and grumbling are like cancer in that it starts small, spreads fast and rots you from within, as well as infecting others around you.

Thomas Brooks said concerning the destructive effects of murmuring: "Murmuring clouds a man's understanding, perverts his judgment, puts out the eye of reason, stupefies his conscience, sours the heart, disorders the will, and distempers the affections. Murmuring makes the life of man invisibly miserable. Every murmurer is his own executioner. Murmuring vexes the heart; it wears and tears the heart, it enrages and inflames the heart, it wounds and stabs the heart. Every murmurer is his own murderer. He kills his joy, comfort, peace, his rest and his soul. He is full of inward gripes and griefs, inward heaviness and bitterness, inward contentions and combustions. He is his own tormentor."

Unlike cancer, murmuring is a communicable disease. As such it is constantly dependent upon carriers that will help transport the disease throughout the Body of Christ.

In the Old Testament we see how this cancer spread its way like wildfire throughout the assembly due to the negative, murmuring, evil report brought back to the congregation by the ten unbelieving spies sent to scout out the Promised Land. It is written, *"All the Israelites grumbled against Moses and Aaron, and the whole assembly said to them, 'If only we had died in Egypt! Or in this desert! Why is the LORD bringing us to this land only to let us fall by the sword? Our wives and children will be taken as plunder. Wouldn't it be better for us to go back to Egypt?' And they said to each other, 'We should choose a leader and go back to Egypt.'"* 13

> *Murmuring is faith out of focus.*

Murmuring is faith out of focus and when this happens to the believer, he begins to see things from a wrong perspective. He begins to zoom in on how unfair life seems to be to some, himself in particular. He begins to notice that it seems as if some people have it all: good looks, intelligence, a good education, an ideal mate, money, popularity, etc. If you find these feelings constantly rising up within your heart, beware, for the clutching hand of envy is attempting to choke from your life all that makes life meaningful and productive. Envy will manifest itself in a judgmental, critical spirit that is always finding fault.

Don't be known as a negative person whose every word is always one of complaining, criticizing, or commiserating over how bad things are.

Make it a practice to be an "affirmer" of people, not a complainer about them. To affirm something is to speak of its positive traits. Affirmation makes the choice to focus on the positive and not the negative. Even if the person or situation is 99 percent negative, focus on the one percent. Affirmation encourages instead of discourages. It builds up instead of blasting to bits. It blesses instead of curses. It refuses flattery but rejoices in finding the slightest good that can be affirmed.

John Mason writes: "A man is wise who does not grieve for the things which he has not, but rejoices for the things which he has. Continually compare what you want with what you have, and you will be unhappy. Instead, compare what you deserve with what you have, and you'll be happy. Decide to stick with love. Envy is too great a burden to bear."

Waiting On God is Waiting in His Place, and Going at His Pace.

If you are anything like me, you have a tendency to pray and ask God for patience. That prayer may sound like this, "Lord, give me patience. And I want it right now." Isaiah said, *"but those who hope in the LORD will renew their strength. They will soar on wings like eagles; they will run and not grow weary, they will walk and not be faint."* [14] Normally when we think about waiting on anybody or waiting on the Lord, we think of progression in a different way than God does. Normally when we think of progression, we think about walking, running, then flying. God's progression for rest is to fly, run, and walk. Here's what He said, *"they that wait on God will mount up with wings as eagles;"* they will fly. Then *"they shall run and not be weary;"* they will run. *"They shall walk and not faint"*; they will walk. So, God reverses it. He does this because He knows what we need. We have need of stability and consistency and longevity in our life. The Christian life is not a fifty yard dash. It is a cross-country, long distance run. We are in this thing for the long haul. God says that we fly, we run, and then we walk. I remember when I first got saved that I was so enthusiastic. I was so passionate that I would witness to anybody and was just consumed with telling folk about Christ. I would

> *We have need of stability, consistency & longevity in life.*

share with everybody that I could. Even when I started preaching, I did a lot of damage because I had passion without wisdom. It was knowledge without grace and I was flying.

I was flying here and there and doing a lot of damage because I was without knowledge and wisdom and maturity. I think that's the way everybody starts out in anything they do in life, with that kind of full bore passion. But then as they grow and mature, they go from flying to running. In other words, they settle down. They become more consistent. They grow. They mature. It's not that they lose their passion or their fire, but it's more directed, more consistent, more settled. After a while, they begin to walk.

Walking is maturity; walking is consistency. Walking is the demonstration that a person has grown in the Lord and grown in life. Now they are doing more good and getting greater results with less effort because they are focused and matured in the Lord. Even James said, *"But the wisdom that comes from heaven is first of all pure; then peace-loving, considerate, submissive, full of mercy and good fruit, impartial and sincere."* [15] In other words, James is saying that when we first learn anything it is pure. It's black and white. I believe in black and white. I believe in absolutes, but sometimes we use those black and white absolutes

Patience is a choice.

as legalism in our life in every area rather than to be full of grace. It's first pure, then peaceable, then gentle, then easy to be entreated. It doesn't mean that we become compromisers. It means that we gain wisdom and mature in the Lord. We learn to negotiate those waters. So remember dear friend, that resting in the Lord and waiting on God is a process. Those that wait on the Lord will renew their strength. Then they will fly. They'll run. Then they will learn to walk. You don't lose your passion. You don't lose your fire. You don't lose your purpose when you are walking. You are just having greater results. Sometimes with a lot less effort, because it's focused passion and purpose.

Waiting on God is moving towards God's will for your life with the "steer-ability" to be guided in another direction when the Holy Spirit reveals it.

John Piper defines waiting on God as "a deepening, peaceful, willingness to wait for God in the unplanned place of obedience, and to walk with God at the unplanned pace of obedience – to wait in His place, and go at his pace."

Jesus declares that those who become successful life-farmers are those who bring forth fruit with patience: *"But the seed on good soil stands for those with a noble and good heart, who hear the word, retain it, and by persevering produce a crop."* [16]

Patience is a choice. Patience is one of the fruit produced from your life tree as you abide in Christ.

The writer of the book of Hebrews reaffirms the words of Jesus as he writes, *"We do not want you to become lazy, but to imitate those who through faith and patience inherit what has been promised."* [17]

He then reiterates this truth, *"You need to persevere so that when you have done the will of God, you will receive what he has promised. For in just a very little while, "He who is coming will come and will not delay."* [18]

"Be patient, then, brothers, until the Lord's coming. See how the farmer waits for the land to yield its valuable crop and how patient he is for the autumn and spring rains." [19]

Waiting On God is Waiting in His Place, and Going at His Pace.

Successful life-farmers are not those who never fail, but like successful dirt farmers, they are those who never quit in spite of droughts, crop failures, seed loss, crop disease, market collapses, equipment breakdown, rising cost, never ending, exhausting work, etc.! They keep on

Stopping at third base adds no more score than striking out!

honoring the laws of the harvest and finally it will come harvest time!

To change metaphors, John Mason reminds us that "stopping at third base adds no more score than striking out. The measure of true success is not just getting a big hit, but making it safely home."

Meanwhile, what are we to do while the harvest tarries?

Our assignment may be in a bad environment, with rough, hard, and ungracious soil. The soil may be saturated with adverse biases, awful prejudices, and unfriendly customs. What shall we do while the harvest tarries? *"Let us not be weary in well doing!"* Yes, and the words have this literal and very searching meaning: *"Let us not be weary in beautiful doing!"* Even if soil is reluctant and ungracious, do not let your labor of love, your service to the Lord, be premature and rude! Let your "doing" be "beautiful" even when you are dealing with unlovely people!

You may say, "that's hard and difficult work!" to do before unlovely people. It's especially hard to go on doing for others when it is unappreciated and thrown away. This demand is apt to strain and tire the spirit! But it's the way to a good harvest. Sowing more evil in return for evil will never produce a good crop.

There is nothing more unwise than to let the cultivation of your garden be neglected because the bit of land you have to till is scraggly and poor. We can make no greater mistake than to become rough and rude just because our audience is rough and rude.

Our sowing, hoeing, watering, weeding and doing must be "beautiful," always and everywhere "beautiful." If the field is hard, let the work be beautiful!

Gazing upon the most evident signs of labor, neatness and finish in his field, one man said to another, "It's by no means easy land, but that's a bit of beautiful work!"

We have by no means been given an easy piece of land down here in our mission, our home, on our job, in our neighborhood, but let our work be beautiful; let our farm be well kept; let every furrow be straight. *"Let us not become weary in doing good, for at the proper time we will reap a harvest if we do not give up."* [20]

One of the Laws of the Harvest states: "We sow in one season; we reap in another." No harvest comes the moment the seed is planted, but it must wait for God's appointed time. This should be both a warning against sowing evil and an encouragement for sowing good seed.

Let us take to heart, and daily keep before us, the words of an old hymn:

Sowing in the morning, sowing seeds of kindness,
Sowing in the noontide and the dewy eve;
Waiting for the harvest, and the time of reaping,
We shall come rejoicing, bringing in the sheaves.
Sowing in the sunshine, sowing in the shadows,
Fearing neither clouds nor winter's chilling breeze;
By and by the harvest, and the labor ended,
We shall come rejoicing, bringing in the sheaves.

Chapter Five:
The Master's Key
to Seeding for Success

Pastor Jack Hayford asks, "Can anything be the key to everything?" He then answers by asserting that giving is the key to everything. His premise for successful life-farming is summed up this way: "Learning and applying the key to everything, i.e. giving, involves the growing of a heart attitude in giving, which gives the right thing at the right time in the right way and for the right reasons."

Why is giving the key to everything? It is because we are never

How we give impacts how we live!

more like our Heavenly Father than when we are living with a giving spirit. How we give impacts how we live!

Here at Restoration Ranch, we have tried to live with an attitude of living to give. One of our mottoes here at the Ranch is: "Live to Give." We know that only as we live to give, can God honor our life in all that we do. In life you will be either a giver or a taker. It's your choice. If you are a taker, then you will never be able to receive enough. If you are a giver, then you will never be able to give enough. God honors those who honor Him. One of the greatest ways to honor God is by living to give.

The Master's Key is not about formulas to make money and get more stuff, although this may be a part of the harvest, but it is about a form of living to give that freely receives God's grace and freely releases it everyday, in everyway, and to everyone!

Give Up your Natural Tendency for Pre-judging and Passing Sentence -- "judge not, condemn not"

Jesus said, *"Do not judge, or you too will be judged. For in the same way you judge others, you will be judged, and with the measure you use, it will be measured to you."*[1] A lot of people assume that this verse means that we must see no evil, speak no evil, and hear no evil as far as sin is concerned. They suppose that we can maintain some sort of neutrality towards sin in the life of another person so as to never make any kind of examination, discrimination, discernment, or judgment. (There are three root words in the Greek translated "judgment" and they all mean to judge, to examine, to critique, to discern).

How are we to respond to the constantly recurring statement, "I thought Christians were not supposed to judge?" Are

> *The truth of the matter is life requires that we make judgments all the time.*

we or are we not to exercise judgment? Yes and no. Yes, we are commended and commanded to judge biblically. No, we are forbidden to judge unbiblically. The truth of the matter is life requires that we make judgments all the time.

Every day we all make judgments in a variety of ways.

Jesus speaking says this concerning judgment: *"Judge not according to appearance."* By this Jesus meant that we are not to critique, judge, and examine on the basis of appearance. However, the remainder of the verse says, *"But judge (there's the commandment) righteous judgment."*

When then is it wrong to judge?

1. When I do so destructively. Judgment is wrong when I engage in destructive criticism; when I aim at destroying, rather than at restoration; when I intend to ruin instead of acting redemptively.

2. When I do so hypocritically. When you and I will not allow in others what we allow in ourselves, then we are involved in sinful, hypo-critical judging. People who are always judging others wrongly are nor-mally guilty of what their favorite judgment is.

Are we guilty of our favorite judgment?

3. When I do so habitually and presumptuously. The people that James was addressing were involved in slandering another person. Slander by definition is truth told about a person designed to hurt their character. Often times we ask people to pray for somebody, but our request is with malice in our heart toward them, only wanting to destroy their character. They were judging presumptuously without evidence, without definite proof; and they were doing so with a spirit that had formed a habit of always passing condemnatory judgment. This is forbidden in scripture. We are not to go off half cocked and say, "Well, I heard the other day ..." and begin to engage in rumors and employ ourselves in developing these suspicions.

We are to do what God did when He said, *"The outcry against Sodom and Gomorrah is so great and their sin so grievous that I will go down and see if what they have done is as bad as the outcry that has reached me. If not, I will know."* [2] Thus we are to make sure that before we render a critique, a judgment, an examination, that we have the facts as best we are able to discern them. But if I do so presumptuously and habitually, then I set myself above the authority of God's Word.

4. When I do so officiously. This type of judgment is outside of my jurisdiction. This belongs to the civil government. I can't judge as a magistrate unless I am a magistrate. I can't judge officiously. There are no vigilantes in the family of God. God alone assigns those jurisdictions.

5. When I judge hastily, rationally, and unmercifully. Judging in this manner involves judging another person's motives. No one, save God, can know another person's motives.

We naturally judge harshly. We tend to always put the worst construction upon what we see and hear about others, and to make small, if any, allowance for the hidden good that is in them. Also, we unwittingly judge others by the worst parts of our own disposition, and not by the best. It's common to impute our evil to others, but to think our goodness is peculiarly our own.

So much of the time when we are unduly harsh or critical with other people, it's because we are venting our own frustrations because we know in our hearts we are not living right before God. Whenever I hear a preacher or a speaker who is being unduly harsh, unduly negative, unduly critical, I know that they are venting their own frustrations about what goes on in their own private life. David, the king of Israel, when found guilty of adultery and murder, was approached by Nathan the prophet. Nathan shared with him the story of a man who had a little ewe lamb, just one! A wealthy man who was a neighbor had a stranger come to visit. It was the custom in those days to take the stranger in, give him a place to sleep and give him a meal. The wealthy man had many sheep in his fold, but instead of taking a sheep from his own fold, he had a servant steal the one little ewe lamb from his neighbor. When Nathan told him of the story of how the man had only one little ewe lamb that he had raised from a baby and that's all he had in life, David was filled with anger. Nathan asked for a judgment of the man who had committed this crime. David, filled with his own guilt, under great conviction, rose up and said this man shall restore four-fold and die.

The strange thing about the story is the law only required that a man should restore four-fold. David went

> *If your heart is full of love, you'll judge in love.*

way beyond the law and said he should also be put to death. David was harsh in his judgment because he had not repented. He himself was filled with his own personal wickedness; he himself had not turned from his sin and was venting his frustrations by being unduly harsh on this particular man.

Nathan finally looked at David, pointed his finger in his face and said, "Behold, thou art the man." Whenever you point your accusing finger at somebody else, there are always three pointing back at you. Remember if your heart's full of love when you judge in a Christ-like way, you'll judge in love and mercy and grace, but when your heart is full of self, sin and flesh, you'll be condemning, slanderous, critical, harsh and unredemptive.

6. It's wrong when we judge minutely. *"Accept him whose faith is weak, without passing judgment on disputable matters."* [3] In other words, don't be judging in minute things that really don't matter. It is this type of activity that we are usually involved in when we judge one another.

Watch out for a judge, jury, and executioner's critical, censorious spirit that is always condemning, castigating, and criticizing, and passing sentence. Guard against a spirit that is filled with pride and envy that is nothing more than disguised hatred. This spirit elevates itself by always putting others down. It appears to make progress when in reality it hasn't gone anywhere. It has just climbed upon the bodies of fallen brothers and sisters.

Forgive those who have Treated You Wrongly -- "forgive and you'll be forgiven"

God intends for His grace to be transmitted from us as freely as it has been given to us.

The word translated forgiveness here is "apoluete." It means *to release.* To forgive is to give up your rights to retribution and revenge and treat with grace and mercy. It means to give over your burdens of bitterness. Forgotten grace breeds unforgiving living.

Forgiveness is a promise made and a price paid. It is a choice of the will. It requires that you absorb all the cost for the offense against you. Have you ever found yourself thinking or saying, "Someone is going to pay for this!" You are absolutely correct -- and you, the one sinned against, are the one who is going to pay! Granting forgiveness means that you pay! It means that you are willing to absorb the loss.

Forgiveness is a full pardon and an act of love. Forgiveness is based upon God's having forgiven you and not simply to get God to forgive you. I came across one of the greatest statements on forgiveness I have ever heard years ago. The statement is simple: forgiveness is your willingness

> *If your heart is full of love, you'll judge in love.*

to bear the consequences of another person's actions or choices. That is what Jesus did for us at the cross when He bore the consequences of our actions and our choices. He did it willingly. The Bible says He endured the cross, but he despised the shame for the joy that was set before Him. That joy was your salvation and mine.

If our forgiveness is to be Christ-like, there must be a willingness to bear the consequences, no matter how difficult, of another person's actions and choices. You may say that's difficult to do, but I tell you it's impossible to do apart from the Spirit of God empowering you and enabling you to make those right choices.

> *Forgiveness is your willingness to bear the consequences of another person's actions or choices.*

Give With Eyes Toward the Prize of the Harvest

What is the prize of the harvest? The joy of becoming more like our Creator, who ever lives to give and forgive!

99

What You Seed is What You Get!

Giving is a consistent lifestyle and not just a weekly law to be observed. Giving isn't a get rich quick scheme where if you run up against a need, you just plant a faith seed and bingo, it's given back 100-fold. And it's not a formula for raising money but for raising men; not for building cash reserves but for building character; it's not a momentary investment plan, but an everyday, in everyway, and to everyone giving-living life-style that declares, *"It's more blessed to give than to receive."* [4] Remember you don't just give to get, because if you just give to get, then you won't get to give. But if you give to get, to give to get, to give to get, then you will get to give. Remember, your life must be a dispenser and not a receptical.

To release our living to its maximum potential requires commanding forth our giving to its fullest possibilities!-- *"freely you have received, freely give."*

There's a giving that is legalistic but produces a lousy harvest! Giving is important, but motive is more important.

"Woe to you, teachers of the law and Pharisees, you hypocrites! You give a tenth of your spices — mint, dill and cummin. But you have neglected the more important matters of the law — justice, mercy and faithfulness. You should have practiced the latter, without neglecting the former." 5

Miserly people are miserable people. Generous people are joyous people!

The Pharisees gave to the religious system but they never gave in to God. They gave up a tenth of everything materially, but they never gave in to the Holy Spirit's correction, direction, and character formation purposes.

A living-giving lifestyle requires an ongoing posture

change toward people as well as toward possessions. Right relationships are what life in the kingdom of God is all about and not just material riches. i.e., things -- "a man's life does not consist of the abundance of things which he possesses."

Let's take a look at the concept of Law and Grace when it comes to the principle of the tithe. The Old Testament is full of law where the New Testament is primarily about grace. The law of giving was designed to lead us to the grace of knowing that God owns it all and allows us to be stewards of what belongs to the King. We are not to give out of obligation or grudgingly. God's desire is for us to be joyful, celebrating the opportunity to sow good seeds. If we sow out of obligation or grudgingly, it has the distinct possibility to taint the given seed. This could yield a less than best harvest. The enemy could use our attitude to rob us of the best seed even in the best soil.

Tithing is a debt you owe... giving is a seed you sow!

In the Old Testament, the Law says to give 10% back to God and His Kingdom. Tithing existed before the Law, so if you want to say we are not under the Law that is okay, but realize that Abraham was giving the tithe pre-law time. So, what does that mean for us now? Well, as I see it, under grace, we are to start where the Law leaves off. Our giving today should start at 10% and go up from there knowing that grace is a higher standard. We are not to move backwards toward the Law, but forward to greater levels of understanding in the grace given by God. Tithing is a debt you owe—giving is a seed you sow.

It's easy to give testimony to the return God has give you on your initial giving to Him and then constantly diminish the level of your giving. For example, a well-known wealthy man rose to address a church meeting. "I'm a millionaire," he said, "and I attribute it all to the rich blessings of God. I remember that turning point in my life. I had just earned my first dollar, and I went to church that Sunday. I knew that I only had a dollar bill and had to either give it all to God's work or give nothing. So at that moment, I decided to give my whole dollar to God. I believe that God blessed that decision, and that is why I am a rich man today."

As he sat down, a little lady sitting in the same pew leaned over and said to him, "Now that you are a millionaire and God has greatly blessed you, I double dog dare you to try it again."

Give to the Size of the Future Harvest

> *Your contribution to others determines God's to you.*

Mike Murdock said, "Your contribution to others determines God's contribution to you. When you let go of what is in your hand, God will let go of what is in His Hand for you." I have always believed: anything God can get through you, God will get to you.

The measure you use to sow reveals the capacity you have to receive. Little cups of grace, mercy, love, kindness, food or money given, mean that you can't receive much in return because you don't have the capacity for it.

Maintaining a Living-Giving Life-style will Result in the Harvest of God Meeting Our Needs -- "seed to the sower and bread for food" 7

Let me reassure you that all God's promises are true. There are Biblical principles that are universal in scope; this means that the Laws of God apply to you no matter if you are in a relationship with God or not. If you give, you will receive.

When Billie and I were starting out in ministry some 37 years ago, there were more times of famine than times of feast. We knew that God would be true to His word if we would only obey His truths. We spent countless thousands of dollars to help the churches and their pastors that we were sent to serve.

During the first revival I preached, the church was small, but had a generous spirit. The offering in 1974 was well over $11,000. That was when $11,000 was almost $11,000. That was a tremendous

God gives seed to sowers, not to hoarders.

amount of money no matter what the generation or year. We took that check and began to sow the good seed into the members of the church we were attending.

We put tires on cars, gave to missions, helped print Bibles, and used a portion to meet our family's needs. We knew that God did not give us that money to hoard, but to sow into others. God gives seed to sowers, not to hoarders. Today God has richly blessed us as a direct result of our sowing in years past. If God can get something through you to others, He will get it to you. God is in the business of expanding us as we empty out all of ourselves. When we are willing to take risks to do for others, God will make a way for us.

Maintaining a Living-Giving Life-style will Result in the Harvest of God Multiplying Our Seed -- "multiply the seed you have sown"

Many years ago, two boys were working their way through Stanford University. Their funds got desperately low, and the idea came to them to engage a great pianist, Padarewski for a piano recital. They would use the funds to help pay their board and tuition. The great pianist's manager asked for a guarantee of $2,000. The guarantee was a lot of money in those days, but the boys agreed and proceeded to promote the concert. They worked hard, only to find that they had grossed only $1,600. After the concert the two boys told the great artist the bad news. They gave him the entire $1,600, along with a promissory note for $400, explaining that they would earn the amount at the earliest possible moment and send the money to him. It looked like the end of their college careers.

> *Those who sow in tears shall reap in joy.*

"No, boys," replied Padarewski, "that won't do." Then tearing up the note, he returned the money to them as well. "Now," he told them, "take out of this $1,600 all of your expenses, and keep for each of you 10 percent of the balance for your work. Let me have the rest."

The years rolled by—World War I came and went. Padarewski, now premier of Poland, was striving to feed thousands of starving people in his native land. There was only one man in the world who could help him, Herbert Hoover, who was in charge of the U.S. Food and Relief Bureau. Hoover responded and soon thousands of tons of food were sent to Poland.

After the starving people were fed, Padarewski journeyed to Paris to thank Hoover for the relief sent him. "That's all right, Mr. Padarewski," was Hoover's reply. "Besides, you don't remember it, but you helped me once when I was a student at college, and I was in trouble. Now that I've been blessed, I'm just paying back the interest." When you are a life-giver and not a life-taker, you never know when and how God's going to pay you back, but it will come. When you cast your bread upon the water, in due season it will come back to you.

Maintaining a Living-Giving Life-style will Result in the Harvest of God Ministering through Our Deeds -- "increase the fruits of our righteousness"

"Those who sow in tears will reap with songs of joy. He who goes out weeping, carrying seed to sow, will return with songs of joy, carrying sheaves with him." [6]

Del Tarr served 14 years in West Africa as a missionary. He saw this principle lived out every year. He writes, "I was always perplexed by Psalm 126 until I went to the Sahel, that vast stretch of savanna just under the Sahara Desert. All the moisture comes in a 4-month period: May, June, July, and August. After that, not a drop of rain falls for 8 months. The ground cracks from dryness, and so do your hands and feet. The year's food, of course, must all be grown in those 4 months. In October and November, the granaries are full from the harvest. People sing, dance and eat two meals a day.

December comes, and the granaries start to recede. Many families omit the morning meal. By January not one family in fifty is still eating two meals a day. By February, the evening meal diminishes. The meal shrinks even more during March and children succumb to sickness. You don't stay well on half a meal a day. April is the month that haunts my memory. In it you hear the babies crying in the twilight. Most of the days are passed with only an evening cup of gruel.

Then, inevitably, it happens. A six or seven-year-old boy comes running to his father with sudden excitement. 'Daddy! Daddy! I found some grain!' he shouts. 'Out in the hut there's a leather sack... Daddy, there's grain in there! Give it to Mommy so she can make flour, and tonight our tummies can sleep!' The father says, 'Son, we can't do that. That's next year's seed grain. It's the only thing between us and starvation. We're waiting for the rains, and then we must use it.' The rains finally arrive in May, and when they do the young boy watches as his father takes the sack from the wall and does

> *I believe in the harvest... therefore I will give what makes no sense.*

the most unreasonable thing imaginable. Instead of feeding his desperately weakened family, he goes to the field and with tears streaming down his face, he takes the precious seed and throws it away. He scatters it in the dirt! Why? Because he believes in the harvest. The seed is his; he owns it. He can do anything with it he wants. The act of sowing the seeds hurts so much that he cries. But as the African pastors say when they preach on Psalm 126, 'Brother and sisters, this is God's law of the harvest. Don't expect to rejoice later on unless you have been willing to sow in tears.'"

Missionary Tarr continues, "And I want to ask you: How much would it cost you to sow in tears? I don't mean just giving God something from your abundance, but finding a way to say, 'I believe in the harvest, and therefore I will give what makes no sense. The world would call me unreasonable to do this -- but I must sow regardless, in order that I may someday celebrate with songs of joy.'"

All our giving must be done in this light: *"For God so loved the world that he gave his one and only Son, that whoever believes in him shall not perish but have eternal life."* [7]

"He who did not spare his own Son, but gave him up for us all — how will he not also, along with him, graciously give us all things?" [8]

God gave His Son in order to get to give you and me the gift of full, free, and forever life in His family.

No life can ever be considered truly successful that hasn't received the gift of eternal life through God's Son. The value of anything depends upon the price paid to purchase it and how long it will last. God paid the ultimate price for you and me when he gave his Son. That transaction will last forever.

What You Seed is What You Get!

Chapter Six:
Managing an Abundant Harvest
The Key to Future Harvest

"Then he said to them, 'Watch out! Be on your guard against all kinds of greed; a man's life does not consist in the abundance of his possessions.' And he told them this parable: 'The ground of a certain rich man produced a good crop. He thought to himself, 'What shall I do? I have no place to store my crops.' Then he said, 'This is what I'll do. I will tear down my barns and build bigger ones, and there I will store all my grain and my goods. And I'll say to myself, 'You have plenty of good things laid up for many years. Take life easy; eat, drink and be merry.' But God said to him, 'You fool! This very night your life will be demanded from you. Then who will get what you have prepared for yourself?' This is how it will be with anyone who stores up things for himself but is not rich toward God." [1]

This study on managing a successful harvest begins by observing a "how-not-to-do-it" type story. Jesus sets forth the illustration in a story that is as old as time and as new as today. It is the parable of a farmer who had an incredibly successful harvest, but failed to manage it scripturally and wisely, and as a result, never got to enjoy any of it.

Jesus prefaced the story by warning that *"a man's life does not consist in the abundance of his possessions"* [2] *"For the waywardness of the simple will kill them, and the complacency of fools will destroy them."* [3]

Character is measured by the management of bumper crops, whether it is in grain or gold, stocks or shops, or from sales or service companies. True success is a life-farming package deal that cannot be segmented into having a lot of money and material things with no time for God or people. A Puritan writer once said, "We ought to make the more careful investments where we are going to spend the longest time. That's not here, but there." The only way that we can make great investments in heaven is to put them in something that's going to span time and eternity... our relationships. That something is not things, but people. Our investment in people via ministries that are helping people, blessing people, rescuing people are ministries that are good soil to plant our seed in.

No person is a success who leaves God out of his life.

William James states that "the greatest use of life is to spend it for something that will outlast it." No person is a success who leaves God out of his life; who neglects his soul; and who leaves eternity out of his planning.

One basic principle of successful life-farming taught by Jesus is: "Don't mistake your body for your soul."

"And I'll say to myself, 'You have plenty of good things laid up for many years. Take life easy; eat, drink and be merry.'" ⁴

The abundant harvest prompted the successful farmer to make plans to enjoy his treasure by indulging in a lifestyle of maximum leisure and pleasure. You will notice in the story of "the rich fool" that no crime is charged to his account; no great evil casts its shadow across his record; no crimson sin stands against him. It is not suggested that he got his wealth illegally or immorally; it is not suggested that it is wrong to have possessions.

Then why did God act so severely toward him when He said, *"This very night your life will be demanded from you. Then who will get what you have prepared for yourself?"*⁵ He had mistaken his body for his soul. God had given him his "soul," his selfhood, for stewardship, and since he had proved unfaithful, God was taking it away from him because he proved himself unfaithful. The rich man thought so persistently about his goods that his life was lost in his livelihood. He forsook the essential for the immediate. His soul was swallowed by the temporal "withouts" that appealed to his body.

Where is the life more abundant promised by our Lord?

What a word for our sensual, body-oriented, sex-driven, if-it-feels-good-do-it, if-it-tastes-good-eat-it, if-it-looks-good-get-it, materialistic society that has much thought for the body and none for the soul. We need to stop and ask, "Where is the life more abundant promised by our Lord?"

In the classic story of <u>Gulliver's Travels</u>, Gulliver is a giant among the tiny Lilliputian pygmies. One day, he awakens to find himself tied down flat to the earth by a thousand little strings. If there had only been one or two, he could have quickly freed himself. But, because there are so many threads, he cannot move. Even so, a human life can be tied down flat and made earth-bound and godless by the stout strings of a thousand things, like this world's goods and petty preoccupations. <u>Gulliver's Travels</u> addresses the same predicament in which the farmer found himself. Both Gulliver and the farmer were bound in earthly things. The eternal things are often neglected.

Cecil Rhodes spent years exploiting the natural resources of South Africa. When he was about to die, he cried out in remorse, "I've found much in Africa.

We should desire to make eternal investments!

Diamonds, gold, and land are mine, but now I must leave them all behind. Not a thing I've gained can be taken with me. I have not sought eternal treasures, therefore I actually have nothing at all."

In our lives, we should desire to make eternal investments. Sow seed that counts for something. That's not to say that we shouldn't address our physical needs. There is no conflict in my mind between leaving an inheritance for our children and storing up treasure in heaven.

Billie and I have always said we want to leave two things for our children when we are gone. First, we want to leave a heritage that represents our relationship with the Lord Jesus Christ. Secondly, we want to leave an inheritance that can further our children and grandchildren financially. But, only that they might be a blessing to the kingdom of God and the work of the kingdom for generations to come. I think it only goes without saying that the spiritual needs of man are the most important needs that man has and to leave a spiritual heritage is the most valuable heritage that parents can leave to their children. About this there is no doubt or argument. However, the work of the kingdom requires resources. Our prayer is that God wills and we steward our resources well that we can leave an inheritance that will make a difference economically and financially in generations to come. We desire to give our children a financial and spiritual spring-board that we never had so they can do great things for God in their lifetime and make a difference in the life of God's people and the people of the world.

A second basic principle of successful life-farming taught by Jesus is: "Don't mistake yourself as being God"

He thought to himself, 'What shall I do? I have no place to store my crops.' Then he said, 'This is what I'll do. I will tear down my barns and build bigger ones, and there I will store all my grain and my goods. And I'll say to myself, "You have plenty of good things laid up for many years. Take life easy; eat, drink and be merry."' [6]

This farmer feels that he is self-made. He basically takes all the credit for the abundant harvest. A closer look at the parable reveals that God is not at all in his thoughts. The counsel he gives and receives is with himself. The focus of attention is I and my. In this man's soliloquy, you will find six I's, five my's, and four I will's. He felt that he was the cap-tain of his destiny, the master of his fate.

The historian of Alcoholics Anonymous (AA) titled his

work "Not-God," because he said that stands as the most important hurdle an addicted person must overcome: to acknowledge, deep in the soul, that they are not God. The founders of AA concluded that " ...the first step to recovery was to quit trying to do God's work and let God be God, which involves daily, moment by moment surrender to Him."

The great theologian Augustine said, "God being God offends human pride." Why? Because if God is running the universe, guess who isn't. Guess who doesn't get to do things his way. By nature we are all little god-players. I can testify personally that it was a grand and glorious day for my loved ones and colleagues when I resigned as general manager of the universe. The older I get there are two truths that I realize more passionately every day: 1) There is a God in heaven. 2) I'm not Him.

> *God being God offends human pride.*

Sin causes man to believe the age-old lie foisted upon man in the Garden of Eden by the Enemy—man can be God. Man believes because he was created in God's image that he is self- sufficient and master of his destiny.

Have you ever heard anyone boast, "I'm a self-made man!" Such a statement only proves the worthlessness of unskilled labor.

A third basic principle of successful life-farming taught by Jesus is: "Don't mistake stewardship for ownership"

Today we have two extremes in respect to possessions. Poverty theology which has a disdain for all possessions and believes they are a curse. Then we have prosperity theology which views possessions as the God-given right of every Christian. Both are wrong. The biblical position is that of stewardship. Possessions are viewed as a trust given in varying proportions that requires wise management for the glory of the Owner, our blessed Lord.

How easy is it to mistake stewardship for ownership? To think in terms of it's mine is to forget who it is that gave you the mind, strength, and opportunity to have what you have. The writer of Proverbs said, *"Keep falsehood and lies far from me; give me neither poverty nor riches, but give me only my daily bread. Otherwise, I may have too much and disown you and say, 'Who is the LORD?' Or I may become poor and steal, and so dishonor the name of my God."*[7] The writer of Proverbs had reason to understand that God knows what our needs are. God knows how to meet those needs.

The writer said, "I don't want to be so full, have so much that I forget where it came from

> *You know God is not against us having wealth.*

and deny the Lord." You know God is not against us having wealth. God is not against us having an increase. What God opposes is when we forget where it came from and forget to acknowledge Him and thank him and be grateful to Him by honoring Him with our resources. Then the writer went on to say, I don't want so little that I have to take the name of the Lord God in vain and steal to get what I need. Now, I know that stealing is never in order and so do you. I weary sometimes of people talking about loving Jesus and not caring about material things. The truth is, we are spiritual beings and that is our highest order of being, but we have physical bodies that live in a material world. I believe that God intends to meet our needs in every area of life, not just one area.

Recently, when I was ministering I had a thought: Paul the Apostle said one way that you prove your love for Jesus is real and goes beyond mere words is by your giving. Some people say, "Well, I just love the Lord and I don't care about material things." If that is true in your life, you are the one God is looking for. You are going to give all or most of your wealth to the Lord because you don't care about material things no matter what your increase, no matter how much you earn. But actually that's not how it usually works out.

Most people that say they love Jesus but don't care about material things are those that give the least to the kingdom of God. Just because a person has wealth doesn't mean they are guilty of the love of money.

> *Just because a person has wealth doesn't mean he is guilty of the love of money.*

Just because a person is skinny or thin, does not mean they are not guilty of the sin of gluttony. Friend, you could have little and be guilty of the love of money. Or you could have much and not be guilty. You could be overweight and not be a glutton. You can be thin and be a glutton. I find when I trust the Lord with all my heart and lean not to my own understanding, I want to be faithful to God. I want to be a good steward over what God gives me. I want God to increase me as it honors Him and pleases Him and blesses Him. I want Him to feed me with food convenient for me.

A fourth basic principle of successful life-farming taught by Jesus is: "Don't mistake time for eternity"

"But God said to him, 'You fool! This very night your life will be demanded from you. Then who will get what you have prepared for yourself? This is how it will be with anyone who stores up things for himself but is not rich toward God.'" [8]

Note the **shortness of his pleasure** -- He thought he could lay up years like he did his goods. Note the **silence of his planning** -- The very first night after his big plans, his soul was required of him in death. And note the **suddenness of his poverty** -- He is classed with fools, cut-off from life, and confined to eternity's poorhouse!

And then, who shall those things be which thou hast provided? This statement has grasped my heart and has grabbed my imagination. One day when reading this statement, God asked me a question. The question was simply this, "Do you think that it is wise to devote and dedicate your life to things that the moment you are gone will belong to somebody else?" The truth is, friend, that we devote and dedicate our lives so much of the time to temporal things that are no more devoted to us than the moment we are gone, they belong to somebody else. This is why this is a great truth and a great teaching—and then, whose shall those things be?

From this teaching of Jesus, we see the need for a proper approach to managing and maintaining the fruitful harvest of the rewards of good sowing. Now that we know what not to do, how are we to handle the abundant harvest?

Successful Management Requires Maintaining Proper Harvest Bins

Harvest Bin # 1 – Setting aside a portion for Philanthropic Exercises

Don't let the big word stump you. Philanthropic is a word that comes from the Greek word **philanthropos** and means loving people. Thus philanthropic exercise is goodwill to fellowmen; an especially active effort to promote human welfare by giving generously.

Feel for others -- in your wallet!

Spurgeon said, "Feel for others -- in your wallet!" However, when it comes to giving, we must be discerning and truly compassionate. The solution to human poverty and problems is not to arbitrarily throw some money at the situation and hope it will go away.

The classic example of a true philanthropic exercise in giving is found in a parable that Jesus told that has come to be known as that of the Good Samaritan.

"In reply Jesus said: 'A man was going down from Jerusalem to Jericho, when he fell into the hands of robbers. They stripped him of his clothes, beat him and went away, leaving him half dead. A priest happened to be going down the same road, and when he saw the man, he passed by on the other side. So too, a Levite, when he came to the place and saw him, passed by on the other side. But a Samaritan, as he traveled, came where the man was; and when he saw him, he took pity on him. He went to him and bandaged his wounds, pouring on oil and wine. Then he put the man on his own donkey, took him to an inn and took care of him. The next day he took out two silver coins and gave them to the innkeeper. 'Look after him,' he said, 'and when I return, I

will reimburse you for any extra expense you may have." 9

How did the Samaritan man in the story treat the person in crisis and need? For starters, he didn't treat his fellow man like a problem, but rather as a human being. The Good Samaritan didn't simply toss the robbery victim some money and proceed blithely on his way. Instead, he did the much more "uncomfortable" task of providing for the person's needs as if they were his own as he *"took him to an inn and took care of him."*

When a person is in need of assistance, the solution is not just to give them material assistance, but to empower them to begin to provide for themselves and to minister to their spiritual needs.

The Good Samaritan is a model of effective compassion, because he

> *Part of being a good steward is giving back to God.*

engages the fallen man as a person; he treats him as his "neighbor." This can at times be inconvenient, costly, and dangerous, and it is rarely simple, but there is no other way to make compassion effective than to follow Christ's command to "Go and do likewise."

Pastor Jack Hayford asks, "Can anything be the key to everything?" He then answers by asserting that giving is the key to everything. His premise for successful life-farming is summed up this way: "Learning and applying the key to everything, i.e. giving, involves the growing of a heart attitude in giving, which gives the right thing at the right time in the right way and for the right reasons."

Part of being a good steward is giving back to God a portion of what He has entrusted to us. It is not that God needs our money. Rather, giving serves as an external, material testimony that God owns both the material and spiritual things of our lives and that He is the source of all our supply.

The first place in Scripture that really directs the tithe states: *"Bring the whole tithe into the storehouse, that there may be food in my house."* [10] In the Old Testament, the storehouse was a physical place where the Jews would deliver their offerings of grain and animals. Ideally, the church should serve as the storehouse in God's economy today.

One day while studying this passage of scripture, I realized that I had missed something for years. In the verses that proceed this verse, God asks His people a question. The question was, *Will a man rob God? Yet you rob me. But you ask, 'How do we rob you?' In tithes and offerings."* [11] Then, God's answer: in tithes and offerings. One day while studying that passage, I realized that there was more to it than just robbing God of tithes and offerings.

I posed the question in my heart to the Lord. "How can a man rob you, God? You don't have need of anything. You really don't need our finances, our resources. You are sufficient in yourself." I feel like the answer that came back to me was so simple, and yet I had missed it for so many years. It was as if God spoke to my heart and said that whenever I disobey the word of God, whenever I rebel against what God has asked me to do, then I rob God of the opportunity of blessing me how He wants to bless me.

God will not accommodate me in my rebellion against His word and bless me in that rebellion. I believe that we have missed the blessings of God in so many areas. I believe that we have robbed God of the opportunity of doing for us what He desires to do. That is exceeding, abundantly above everything we can ask or think. As it were, we have tied God's hands from His gracious blessings because of our rebellion.

If we are not being blessed in areas of our life today, it may be that we need to examine ourselves and try to be honest about the areas of our life where we may be in rebellion against God. He wants to bless us. He wants to enlarge our tents and lengthen our cords. He wants to increase us. He wants us to grow and mature. But we only experience the blessings of God in proportion to our obedience to Him. Every promise of God has a condition with it. When I meet His conditions, God will fulfill His promises. The more God increases me, the more God expects from me. To whom much is given, much shall be required.

> *Giving is not about problems or poverty but PRIORITIES.*

Irrespective of the size of the harvest, a portion should always be set aside for the tithe which God demands and for the offerings which He deserves.

Here are Four Great Truths About Giving.

1. Giving is not about problems or poverty but PRIORITIES. We will always have pressures, problems, hardships, and heartaches. Our enemy will always supply us with a reason to be selfish. But rest assured, when we allow our problems, pains, and our greedy, stingy attitudes control our stewardship, we limit God's ability to bless us.

2. Giving is not about wealth but WILLINGNESS. Giving has nothing to do with how much you have but what you do with what you have. Remember the widow's mite? Jesus said,

"I tell you the truth," he said, "this poor widow has put in more than all the others. All these people gave their gifts out of their wealth; but she out of her poverty put in all she had to live on."[12]

3. Giving is not about obligation but OPPORTUNITY. Timing is everything in giving. To delay until tomorrow what God expects you to do today is to rob your act of giving of its full intent and impact. Many defer their giving until they are dead. They say in essence to God, "We will now give you something that we can no longer keep."

4. Giving is not about legalism but LORDSHIP. We learn that the people in Corinth *"...they gave themselves first to the Lord and then to us in keeping with God's will."* [13] First, they settled the issue of ownership, i.e. who's the Boss, and how much does he own? Then it was no problem for them to give all they had to Jesus and then to trust Him for a miracle to be able to give help to those in need. When you've settled the Lordship issue, you stop quibbling about the small stuff.

> *Many people believe that one should give until it hurts. The problem with this is that most people are far too sensitive to pain!*

We should give because we believe that Jesus Christ is Lord and deserves our best, not because we feel as though we have to.

Many people believe that one should give until it hurts. The problem with this is that most people are far too sensitive to pain! The Scriptures teach that to give grudgingly is sad giving

> *The cure for greed is in the seed.*

and that necessity type giving is mad giving, but cheerful giving is glad giving!

We must understand that kingdom economics is investing in the fulfillment of the Great Commission prompted by the grace of the Great Commandment. We must stop merely giving to help others out and start investing wisely in people, and the things that enable us to reach, teach, and equip world-visionary, world-impacting, reproducing life-long followers of King Jesus!

"If you are willing to start giving where you are with what you have, then God won't leave you where you are and He will increase what you have."

Always remember, God will provide seed for the sower.

If you will give, God will see to it that you have an abundance to plant again.

John Wesley taught his disciples to make all they could, give all they could, and save all they could!

Harvest Bin # 2 – Setting aside a portion for Personal Enjoyment

"The hardworking farmer should be the first to receive a share of the crops." [14] Paul is saying that the right of first partaking of the fruits of the harvest belongs to him who is laboring, so in that light, work hard and expect to be the first one to enjoy the benefits of your labors.

Don't let a lifetime pass by before you begin enjoying the fruits of your labor.

Philip Parham tells the story of a rich industrialist who

was disturbed to find a fisherman sitting lazily beside his boat. "Why aren't you out there fishing?" he asked.

"Because I've caught enough fish for today," said the fisherman.

"Why don't you catch more fish than you need?' the rich man asked.

"What would I do with them?"

"You could earn more money," came the impatient reply, "and buy a better boat so you could go deeper and catch more fish. You could purchase nylon nets, catch even more fish, and make more money. Soon you'd have a fleet of boats and be rich like me."

The fisherman asked, "Then what would I do?"

"You could sit down and enjoy life," said the industrialist.

The fisherman just grinned and said, "That's exactly what I'm doing now!"

One person tells of having a dream that they had an interview with God:

"So you would like to interview me?" God asked.

"If you have the time," I said.

God smiled, "My time is eternity. What questions do you have in mind for me?"

"What surprises you most about humankind?"

God answered, "That they get bored with childhood, they rush to grow up, and then long to be children again. That they lose their health making money... and then lose their money to restore their health. That by thinking anxiously about the future, they forget the present, such that they live in neither the present or the future. That they live as if they will never die, and die as though they had never lived."

Dennis Waitley shares a personal illustration that stresses the importance of viewing everyday above ground as a good day and enjoying the fruits of the harvest today: "I will never forget one Friday in the Chicago O'Hare Airport. I had just finished speaking and was anxious to get home to my family in California, so I could spend another day, another week, and another month on the road. I seemed to be chasing life at that time. I hurried to the gate, from which my plane was scheduled to depart, but by the time I arrived, the door had closed, and the airplane was pulling back from the gate. It was a DC-10. Flight 191.

In a little over an hour later, a broken bolt would give way on that plane. The wing pod would fall off, and the plane would crash, with great loss of life.

To this day, I keep that invalidated ticket on Flight 191 to remind me to enjoy a portion of all life's harvests as they are reaped. When I get angry or frustrated from time to time, my wife will pull out that ticket and ask simply, 'What are you grousing about today?' I look at my ticket, I look at my life, and I must conclude, 'Nothing.' Every day is Christmas and every day is Easter to me."

Harvest Bin # 3 – Setting aside a portion for Potential Emergencies in the Future

Good News Connection: "About 5 percent of net spendable income should be put aside in an emergency reserve savings, to take care of expenses that cannot be anticipated."

Unexpected expenses are not only bitter disappointments, but they can cause a painful realization if people do not have funds set aside to cover the expenses. *"The rich rule over the poor, and the borrower is servant to the lender."*[15] Even if emergency savings have been set aside, there is little escape from personal or family difficulties resulting from financial emergencies. But when there are crises or unexpected emergencies, much frustration can be avoided if an emergency savings account has been established to help absorb the ordeal of the crisis.

Families should work toward setting aside an amount equal to three to six months salary for emergency savings for those who have a steady income; and for those who have a fluctuating or seasonal income, six months salary is best. This does not mean that large amounts of money should be saved while failing to pay creditors, but a good habit to develop is to save a small amount on a regular basis.

The parable of the ant says; *"Go to the ant, you sluggard; consider its ways and be wise! It has no commander, no overseer or ruler, yet it stores its provisions in summer and gathers its food at harvest."* [16] Within their colony, ants have calculated almost exactly what they will need to get through the winter. They gather and store that amount in their anthill during the summer and autumn.

The need for contingency funds

There are two reasons why families need contingency funds: for emergencies, and for major expenditures.

Emergencies. A contingency fund is first an emergency fund for dealing with the unexpected. By having this money set aside and readily available, emergencies can be paid for without having to borrow.

Major expenditures. A contingency fund also can be used to finance major expenditures that are not in the family operating budget: replacing an old car, buying furniture, replacing appliances, or remodeling.

Whether contingency funds are used for emergencies or for major expenditures, a good rule to follow is that whenever funds are withdrawn from contingency accounts every effort should be made to rebuild the fund as quickly as possible.

The need for insurance funds

Life insurance. The Bible teaches that a man that does not provide for his own is worse than an infidel. I believe that is not only in life, but in death. I believe that includes not only in his spiritual life, but also in his material life. The responsible party is obligated before God to provide for his own. I believe this means that he should take care of his family in the event of his death. Life insurance is an awesome way to provide this benefit and blessing to his family. It's good to get with a financial planner, life insurance agent, or somebody to make sure that should you die, your family will be well provided for.

Health insurance. Costs are rising today for medical bills. That is why I also believe that a good major medical policy, if you are not provided one through your employer, should be set in place to protect yourself from any financial ruin in your future.

How much should be allocated?

Families should allocate a percentage of their income to

contingency funds. Although 10 percent is preferred, a minimum of 5 percent of Net Spendable Income should be placed in contingency funds.

Even though some financial planners recommend keeping a specific amount (like $10,000 for example) in contingency funds, most planners recommend maintaining a minimum of

Honor God by honoring your debts.

three to six months of living expenses for families who have steady incomes; for those who have fluctuating or seasonal incomes, six months living expenses is best.

Again, this does not mean that large amounts of money should be saved while failing to pay creditors, but a good habit to develop is to save on a consistent basis. Remember those that honor God, He will honor. Honor God by honoring your debts that you have created. A good goal for everybody is to work toward being debt free in every area. Owe no man anything, but to love him. It's an honorable, worthy goal for all of us to aim for.

Harvest Bin # 4 – Setting aside a portion for Profitable Expansion

Scripturally sound reasons to invest

• That God might give you greater seed for a future harvest.

• For expansion of future business. I pastor an organization, World Wide Dream Builders, who has the greatest support system for people who are building their own businesses of any support system I have ever observed anywhere. World Wide has not only a great staff to support and underwrite every independent business owner, but also supplies books, cds, functions, mentorship and teaching seminars that are unrivaled. When a person is building their own business, they must be educated. They must have the proper tools. They must have the proper encouragement and mentorship, if they are going to do great things with that business. There is little doubt that those that are willing to pay the price and make the sacrifice to invest in these tools and opportunities are able to insure the greatest possibility of success for their life and for their future business.

• Multiply to give more. Jesus' parable of the talents tells us that God entrusts wealth to some of His stewards so that it will be available to Him at a later date. Wealth management requires that it be invested or multiplied.

• Meet future family needs. God's Word indicates that the heads of families should provide for their own. Good planning requires laying aside some surplus for future needs.

• Further the Gospel and fund special needs. This giving is necessary to maintain and promote the Gospel. If the church is ever to break out of the borrowing habit, Christians who invest must maintain some surpluses and be willing to give to legitimate needs.

Unsound reasons to invest

• Greed. The desire to continually have more and demand only the best.

• Envy. The desire to achieve based on other people's successes.

• Pride. The desire to be elevated because of material achievements.

What You Seed is What You Get!

• Ignorance. Lack of discernment in following the counsel of others.

Remember it's all a matter of stewardship. God holds us responsible and accountable. Our investments in this life will reflect our relationship with Christ.

Chapter Seven:
How to Handle Crop Failures

In any type of farming, crop-failures are inevitable. There are a plethora of things that can cause crop-failure, and often the events are totally beyond the farmer's control.

This holds true in life-farming as well. Successful life-farmers are those who understand that crop-failures are unavoidable. However, the difference between success and failure is determined by how quickly one learns that failures do not have to be final, fruitless, or fatal. In addition, successful life-farming will be determined by how quickly one learns the art of replanting and resists the temptation to quit without re-sowing good seed. Trying times are not time to quit trying.

Napoleon Hill, in his famous book "Think and Grow Rich" reveals the seed factor that is present in every crop-failure: "Every adversity, every failure and every heartache carries with it the seed of an equivalent or a greater benefit."

We learn from Zig Ziglar the tragic result of accepting failure as final. He tells a story in his book, "See You At The Top," concerning putting fleas in a jar with a lid on it. Immediately, the fleas begin to jump up and hit that top in an attempt to get out. But then after about 20 minutes, a strange thing happens. They don't jump as high any more since they know there is a lid there and they can't possibly get out. At that point, you can take the lid completely off. With a perfectly clear path to freedom, those little fleas will starve to death in that jar because they believe there is no way out. We are like these fleas at times. After trying and trying, we stop because we feel there is no hope. Ivan Corbett was a prize fighter. When asked what he felt was his secret of success, the answer he gave was, "Fight one more round. Never give up. Keep on fighting." Or in other words, keep on sowing good seed!

Every adversity, every failure and every heartache carries with it the seed of an equivalent or a greater benefit.

Research shows us that entrepreneurs fail an average of 3.8 times before they finally make it in a business venture. They recognize that three steps forward and two steps backward still have a net result of one step of progress. If you can decide to see your own failures as a necessary part of your progress, you will separate yourself from the average person and put yourself into the category of a potential high achiever.

Thomas Edison was an inquisitive child at an early age. Yet he attended school for only three months where the teacher labeled him "too stupid to learn anything." He was fired from his first two jobs for being "non-productive." As an inventor, Edison made over 10,000 unsuccessful attempts to invent the light bulb. When a reporter asked, "How did it feel to fail 10,000 times?" Edison replied, "I didn't fail 10,000 times. The light bulb was an invention with 10,000 steps." In doing this, Edison discovered 10,000 ways how not to build a light bulb.

Walt Disney never graduated from high school. After a stint as a Red Cross ambulance driver in WWI, Walt worked for a local company in Kansas City. Walt was once fired by a newspaper editor because "he lacked imagination and had no good ideas." In his spare time he made his own cartoons called "Laugh-O-Grams." He saved enough money to start his own company by eating only once a day and slept in his office at night. The Disney company he started, after seven failures, continues to grow with sales of over $12 billion annually and over 100,000 employees.

- The first time stand-up comic Jerry Seinfeld walked out on stage at a comedy club as a professional comic, he looked out at the audience, froze, and totally forgot how to talk. He stumbled through "a minute and a half" of material and was booed off the stage.

- Winston Churchill failed the 6th grade.

- Director Steven Spielberg dropped out of high school in his sophomore year. He was persuaded to come back and was placed in a learning-disabled class. He lasted a month and dropped out of school forever.

- In 1954, the manager of the Grand Ole Opry fired Elvis Presley after one performance. He told Presley, "You ain't goin' nowhere, son. You ought to go back to drivin' a truck."

Don't be like Charlie Brown in how you respond to failure. In one segment, he had just built a beautiful sand castle. As soon as he stood back to admire his masterpiece, it gets flattened by a huge wave. Staring at the now smooth spot where his day's work had been moments before, he says, "There must be a lesson here, but I don't know what it is."

> *Learn from your failure. See it as a stepping stone toward the success you ultimately want.*

Don't accuse God of blocking you. *"Consider it pure joy, my brothers, whenever you face trials of many kinds, because you know that the testing of your faith develops perseverance. Perseverance must finish its work so that you may be mature and complete, not lacking anything."* [1]

"Many of life's failures are people who did not realize how close they were to success when they gave up." -- Thomas Edison

"Failure is the opportunity to begin again more intelligently." -- Henry Ford

"Failure is one of the most important and necessary steps in moving forward." --Paul Tsika

God alone can turn our greatest failures into our greatest successes. Why, you ask? Simply to demonstrate and make know His manifold wisdom to all the universe. *"His intent was that now, through the church, the manifold wisdom of God should be made known to the rulers and authorities in the heavenly realms,"* [2]

At the end of last semester, an arrogant student complained about how he failed the spelling course. The teacher invited him to write a formal letter of complaint to the principal. The teacher glanced at his letter to see how it was going. His first sentence read, "Dear Principle, it is infair and unposible that I faled spelling."

The Christian Science Monitor says that in Berlin, Germany, a man failed his driver's test in 1961 and never tried to retake it. Since then he's been busy working as a driving instructor.

"Without the rocks, the stream would lose its song."
-- a Proverb

"If you stumble, make it part of the dance."

Some have the philosophy, "if at first you don't succeed, destroy all evidence that you ever tried." Just remember, many fail because they take the path of least resistance while laboring with the least persistence.

Many fail because they take the path of least resistance while laboring with the least persistence.

In all probability the failures that come to one's mind when they hear the word used in regards to life issues are basically moral in nature and occur because of sins committed or bad seed sown. This may or may not be the case. There are many who are moral and upright and have sown good seeds in good soil only to experience such miserable failure that they have vowed to never try again. But all great people have all kinds of crop-failures! I want to emphasize as many times as necessary, the only time failure is final is when you let it be.

Every Man Falls and Fails Frequently --
Even a Righteous Man!

Even the Best of Sowers, Using the Best of Seeds, in the Best of Soils, Still has to Deal with Crop-failures and Counterfeiters that Attempt to Choke out the Harvest

Proverbs teaches us that a just man falls seven times, but rises again. The unjust fall and stay down.

Don't give your attention to the seed that never produced the desired crop. Don't be overly concerned about the "weeds" or imitation wheat. If you continue to do what's right, what's wrong and who's wrong will eventually leave your life.

W. A. Ward said, "Failure should be our teacher, not our undertaker. Failure is delay, not defeat. It is a temporary detour, not a dead end street."

The Liabilities of Past Crop-Failures Require Evaluation and Elimination

We must use Heaven's Farming Methods in order to eliminate the bad seed and disseminate the good. *"He also said, "This is what the kingdom of God is like. A man scatters seed on the ground. Night and day, whether he sleeps or gets up, the seed sprouts and grows, though he does not know how. All by itself the soil produces grain—first the stalk, then the head, then the full kernel in the head. As soon as the grain is ripe, he puts the sickle to it, because the harvest has come."* [3]

We must learn the "dung" principle of spiritual farming. *"What is more, I consider everything a loss compared to the surpassing greatness of knowing Christ Jesus my Lord, for whose sake I have lost all things. I consider them rubbish, that I may gain Christ."* [4]

We must learn that whatever "stinking" portion of our past crop-failures that can't be thrown out can nevertheless be turned into fertilizer for future harvests.

Eliminate all your regrets over crop-failures for they are an appalling waste of energy. You can't plant any seed in the soil of regret. Regret is only good for wallowing in.

Find a reason why you can replant good seed for a future harvest, instead of regretting that you didn't.

Eliminate all your regrets over crop-failures for they are an appalling waste of energy.

"If only" and "I can't" are two seeds that, if continually sown, will insure that your life will be a crop-failure.

Eliminate the seeds of unhealthy shame, and the seeds of undeserving blame, and the same seeds that failed to germinate in the last planting. Begin to sow the seeds that have the pattern to produce the harvest God has for you!

Life can sometimes be understood backwards, but it must always be lived forwards. Look backwards with gratitude to God in that although your past seemed like "hell on earth," you weren't sentenced to "hell under the earth!" Then look forward with confidence that the prospects of your future are as bright as the promises of God!

Remember God doesn't review your past in order to determine your future.

For a righteous man may fall seven times and rise again! But unsuccessful people in life are those who fail or never attempt to get up.

Never Judge Apparent Success by Outward Appearance

A vampire bat came flapping in from the night covered in fresh blood and parked himself on the roof of the cave to get some sleep. Pretty soon all the other bats smelled the blood and began hassling him about where he got it. He told them to go away and let him get some sleep, but they persisted until finally he gave in. "OK, follow me," he said and flew out of the cave with hundreds of bats behind him. Down through a valley they went, across a river and into a forest full of trees. Finally he slowed down and all the other bats excitedly gathered around him. "Now, do you see that tree over there?" he asked. "Yes, yes, yes!" the bats all cried in an excited frenzy. "Good," said the first bat, "because I didn't!"

Listen, what has the visible marks of success often times is the blood of our own failures!

Michael Jordan, early in life, looked like a failure at sports. In fact he was cut from his high school basketball team. After an incredibly successful career in basketball, he said in a commercial tribute to him, "I've missed more than 9,000 shots in my career. I've lost almost 300 games. 26 times I've been trusted to take the game winning shot and missed. I've failed over and over and over again in my life. And that is why I succeed."

A new employee asked a bank president, "Sir, what is the secret to your success?" The banker replied, "Right decisions." "And how do you make right decisions?" The banker confidently said, "Experience." "And how do you get Experience?" The banker honestly said, "Wrong Decisions."

Abraham Lincoln failed in business, lost numerous elections and his sweetheart. He even had a nervous breakdown.

But he never quit. He kept on trying. According to many, he became our greatest president. Dr. Seuss' first children's book was rejected by 23 publishers. Henry Ford failed and went broke five times before he finally succeeded.

My son, Paul Edward, failed first grade and fourth grade. He dropped out of school in the tenth grade and got his GED. But, God sent him to college and seminary. He now has his Masters in Christian Education. Not bad for a son who hated school. He is the most educated of all our children.

Napoleon Bonaparte graduated 42nd in a class of 43. Then he went out and conquered Europe. Maybe grades don't matter that much. You may have done poorly in school. God can still use you. Please don't misunderstand what I am saying. I am very pro-education. I know God can hit a lick with a crooked stick; but I also know that God can hit a lick with a straight stick. I believe in getting all the education you can get, but then realize that wisdom comes from God. Education without God's wisdom is like a horse without a rider. It may look great, but it will never accomplish very much.

Babe Ruth hit 714 home runs during his career but he also struck out 1,330 times. Nobody talks about that. He struck out almost twice as many times as he hit home runs. Yet, he once said, "Never let the fear of striking out keep you from taking a swing at the ball." Some times we're so afraid of failure, we're never going to succeed because we don't try. Or we try something, then we give up. We don't hang on. We don't hang in there. But that's how we get good at something. We've got to fail in order to succeed.

Highly successful English author John Creasy received 753 rejection slips from publishers who wouldn't publish his books. But at the same time he published 564 books in his lifetime. He wouldn't let rejection stop him. If someone didn't like it, he'd try somewhere else.

R. P. Macy, the guy who founded Macy's department store, failed seven times at retailing – seven bankruptcies before he started Macy's. He was obviously a big success.

The Responsibilities of the Present Crop Re-Seeding Requires Information and Perspiration

Genius is one percent inspiration and ninety-nine percent perspiration. Good life-farming is biblical information and holy perspiration. Whatever you do, do hardily as unto the Lord.

We must never rest on the laurels of a few good crops -- "He who rest on his laurels gets knocked on his rear end!"

If ever we want a delivery, there must be a period of labor!

Labor isn't so much doing things as delivering hidden stuff.

Work as though your life depends upon it because it does!

Every job is working for you. How? It teaches you discipline and reveals character flaws that you can fix. It helps you to discover the satisfaction of accomplishment and the results of perseverance. God gives you work to activate your power. Nothing is more exhausting than searching for easy ways to make a living!

Remember Work Expands your Resources. Faithfulness over little things brings larger responsibilities and more work, which brings more resources to work with. *"Whoever can be trusted with very little can also be trusted with much, and whoever is dishonest with very little will also be dishonest with much. So if you have not been trustworthy in handling worldly wealth, who will trust you with true riches? And if you have not been trustworthy with someone else's property, who will give you property of your own?"* [5]

Stop wishing and start willing and working. Stop proposing and start purposing. Stop procrastinating and start planning. Stop the self-pity over crop-failure and begin to sow for a future harvest!

There are three possible responses to Crop-failures --

(1) Cover up and react by blaming others in general and God in particular for the consequences of your choices!

(2) Give up and return in unbelief to the old sinful ways of the past!

(3) Stand up and respond to God with faith in His forgiveness and begin to re-sow good seed for a good harvest in your life.

In order to respond to God in faith, we must plant correctly. Some seeds have a short shelf-life and must be sown before the expiration date. Delayed obedience is disobedience. You cannot do the right thing too soon,

Remember you can't make wrong, work.

for you never know when it will be too late. Trying to do the right thing when the door of opportunity is closed is like trying to board a bus that has already left.

In order to respond to God in faith, we must cultivate consistently. If you feed faith it grows; if you feed your doubts, they grow. You must add to your faith.

In order to respond to God in faith, we must give constant attention. We don't have to plant weed seed. The weeds grow all by themselves. We must constantly attend our field to keep weeds from taking over.

In order to respond to God in faith, we must multiply our prayer time. Divide the truth from a lie, subtract negative influences, and add God's Word. Remember you can't make wrong work. Never chase a lie: if you leave it alone, it will run itself to death. You must weed out the lies and live truthfully and speak truthfully. A lie will add to your troubles, subtract from your energy, multiply your difficulties, and divide your effectiveness. Life is always an uphill battle for those who aren't on the level.

We must be positive on God's negatives – All of God's "thou shall nots" are designed for safety and success.

We must learn the power of a positive "No!" -- Learn to say "no" to the good so you can say "yes" to the best. There are two quick ways to disaster: taking nobody's advice and taking everybody's advice.

We must not rejoice when our enemies fail and fall -- *"Do not gloat when your enemy falls; when he stumbles, do not let your heart rejoice,"* [8]

We must know that even our failures are in a much larger plan that can't ultimately fail! - *" If the LORD delights* *in a man's way, he makes his steps firm; though he stumble, he will not fall, for the LORD upholds him with his hand."* [7]

Remember crop-failure is an event that you experience and it doesn't define you or confine you to the field of being a failure!

This is a very interesting response from a lady in Louisville, KY when asked on her 93rd birthday what she would do differently if she had her life to live over:

"If I had my life to live over, I would dare to make more mistakes next time. I would relax. I would limber up. I would be sillier than I've been this time. I would take fewer things seriously, and I would take more chances. I'd take more trips; I'd climb more mountains and swim more rivers. I would eat more ice cream, and fewer beans. I would perhaps have more actual troubles, but I'd have fewer imaginary ones.

> *Remember crop-failure is an event that you experience and it doesn't define you or confine you to the field of being a failure!*

You see, I am one of those people who lived sensibly and sanely, hour after hour, day after day. Oh, I've had my moments, but if I had it to do over again, I'd have more of them. In fact, I'd try to have nothing else - just moments - one after another instead of living so many years ahead.

I've been one of those persons who never goes anywhere without a thermometer, a hot-water bottle, a raincoat, and a parachute. If I had my life to live over, I would go barefoot earlier in the spring, and I would stay that way later in the fall. I would go to more dances. I would ride more merry-go-rounds. I would pick more daisies." --Nadine Stair

What would you do differently if you had the opportunity to live your life over? Why not start doing those things now?

John Johnson, founder of Ebony and Jet magazines, used his mother's furniture as collateral and borrowed $500 in 1942 to launch a publishing business. As an African American, he never used excuses for lack of success. Here's a quote of his that I have used for many years: "Men and women are limited, not by the place of their birth, not by the color of their skin, but by the size of their hope." His worth is estimated at $350 million.

> *Men and women are limited not by the place of their birth, not by the color of their skin, but by the size of their hope.*

Kenneth Taylor, founder of Tyndale House in Wheaton, Illinois, loved the Bible but found the King James version difficult for his children. So, he paraphrased some of the stories and found that his children grasped the principles much easier. Utilizing the time on his train ride each morning into Chicago, he then created *The Living Bible*. Although he had a strong reputation in publishing already, no one would publish this new Bible. So he created his own publishing company. The Living Bible has now sold over 40 million copies in the US alone and Tyndale House is a $100 million dollar company.

"Don't wait for extraordinary opportunities. Seize common occasions and make them great." —Orison Swett Marden

"Far better is it to dare mighty things, to win glorious triumphs, even though checkered by failure, than to rank with those poor spirits who neither enjoy much nor suffer much, because they live in a gray twilight that knows not victory nor defeat." —Theodore Roosevelt

"Sometimes I lie awake at night, and I ask, 'Where have I gone wrong?' Then a voice says to me, 'This is going to take more than one night.'" —Charlie Brown (Peanuts comic strip)

"If you want to know my identity, don't ask me what I do or where I work. Rather, ask me what kind of person I'm becoming or how I'm fulfilling my purpose in life." —Dan Miller

"No one is a failure who truly understands and lives out who they are in Christ and who Christ is in them." —Paul Tsika

One of the greatest challenges people have in life is that they try to get their identity from someplace other than in Christ. If you are trying to get your identity and sense of purpose from your money, from your position, from your pin level or from your relationships, you will always come up short. But, if you get your sense of worth and value and identity from who you are in Christ and who Christ is in you, you will always be triumphant and victorious.

In the modern "busyness" of modern life, I fear we have lost the rhythm between activity and rest. Just as exhaling without occasionally inhaling will cause you to turn blue and pass out, busyness without rest will cause you to "pass out" from things that matter. "I am so

> *No one is a failure who truly understands and lives out who they are in Christ and who Christ is in them.*

busy." We say this as a badge of honor, as if our exhaustion were a trophy, and our ability to withstand 70-80 hour work weeks a mark of real character. We convince ourselves that the busier we are, the more we are accomplishing and the more important we must be. But is this really so? Does more activity really mean more accomplishment? To be unavailable to friends and family, to miss the sunsets and the full moons, to blast through all our obligations without time for taking a deep breath - this has become the model of a successful life.

Through the years of ministering to people in churches and those in the business world, I have seen many people burn up and many burn out. I believe the reason for all this is very subtle, yet very simple, because it is the work that kept them going and not God Himself. Is He the center of all our activity? If not, we will become weary in well doing. Is He what our lives are all about? If not, we will fall by the wayside. God Himself must be the center of all our activity. Christ Himself must be the one who motivates us, encourages us and challenges us to greater life.

Can we really separate ourselves from things that matter in our efforts to get more things? Just this week I worked with a very competent lady who has reached the pinnacle in her profession. She has a world class apartment and a lake house for the weekends. Although her income puts her in the top 1% nationally, she has lost the sense of fulfillment at work. One of her expressed goals is to "smile more on my way to happiness." I fully believe in being sold out to your dream, but for many, their dreams have turned into a nightmare because of misplaced priorities.

Embrace Sabbath days and times in your life. Wisdom, peace, contentment and insight about fulfilling work will grow in those times. Take a walk. Give thanks for simple things. Take a bath with music and candles. Turn off the cell phone, pager, TV and computer. Carve out those times for restoration and spiritual breathing.

A miser, to make sure of his property, sold all that he had and converted it into a great lump of gold. He hid his lump of gold in a hole in the ground, and went continually to visit and inspect it. This roused the curiosity of one of his workmen, who, suspecting that there was a treasure, when his master's back was turned, went to the spot and stole it away. When the miser returned and found the place empty, he wept and tore his hair. A neighbor who saw him in this extravagant grief, upon learninig the cause of it, said, "Fret thyself no longer, but take a stone and put it in the same place, and think that it is your lump of gold; for as you never meant to use it, the one will do you as much good as the other."

Moral of the story: The worth of money is not in its possession, but in its use.   *Aesop Fable, Sixth Century B.C.*

The same is true of talents and abilities. Just knowing you have the ability means nothing. It is only in finding an application that there is any benefit for you or the world. What gold lump are you using for no more benefit than what any common stone would provide?

I beg you my dear friend to use your "gold lump" today as the catalyst of sowing good seed into good soil, so God will allow you to have a good harvest with eternal consequences. Now, let's go seeding.

A French theologian, at the end of his life, talked of his dying regrets. In sharing with us some of his greatest regrets, he admitted that he had been a man preoccupied with petty interests. No matter how much one earns, no matter how much one accomplishes, no matter how much one achieves in this life, every believer has one passion, one purpose and that is to hear the Lord say, *"Well done, thou good and faithful servant."* I think this is why this French theologian offered this advice. "Beware of the barrenness of a busy life." You can be busy and be barren. For whatever we do in word and deed, we do to the glory of God.

Chapter Eight:
Seven Irrefutable Laws of the Harvest

As long as earth remains, God has promised that seedtime and harvest shall be in effect. No person can mock God by altering or circumventing His laws or principles of the harvest. This truth is designed to have either an encouraging or discouraging impact on the way we live our lives. We are encouraged by discovering that if we learn to cooperate with God's laws of the harvest and sow good seed in good soil, then we can in due time expect an abundant harvest of good fruit. Even the discouraging factor in the laws can be very positive and productive. It serves to remind us that if we sow bad seeds or fail to properly care for the seeds sown, then we will reap the prolific harvest of the negative, the painful, and the poisonous fruits that such choices produce.

Failure to understand the seven basic laws of the harvest is a major reason why so many people *"sow the wind and reap the whirlwind."* [1] It is not enough to be sincere, zealous and hard-working if you are ignorant of the truths of sowing and reaping.

What You Seed is What You Get!

This is illustrated by the tale of a city slicker who moves to the country after graduating from college and decides he is going to take up farming. He heads to the local co-op and tells the man, "Give me 100 baby chickens." The co-op man complies. He planted the chicks head first and they all died. A week later the man returns and says, "Give me 200 baby chickens." The co-op man complies. He planted the chicks feet first and they all died.

Again, a week later the man returns. This time he says, "Give me 500 baby chickens." "Wow!" the co-op man replies, "You must really be doing well!"

"Naw," said the man with a sigh, "The last two crops all died!"

Upon learning that the city slicker was an alumnus of Texas A&M, the co-op manager suggested that he write their agriculture department and ask for their counsel. He did and a few weeks later received a registered letter which he quickly signed for and then ripped open. It read, "Dear Alumnus, Thank you for your letter of inquiry. Please send a soil sample as soon as possible." You can have all the zeal possible, but if you don't know the truth, it can't set you free. Not only must we pay attention to the concepts of the harvest, but to the counsel we receive as well!

Pat Robertson refers to these concepts of the harvest as the "Laws of Reciprocity." This natural law of reciprocity does not just apply exclusively to plants and trees. There are many types of seeds that can be sown. There are the seeds of love, seeds of friendliness, seeds of mercy, seeds of money and material blessings of others, etc. On and on the list can go. All of these "giving of yourself" type seeds, after they are sown in the ground, can begin to produce quite a large harvest, as well. Someone expressed it like this: If you want to be rich...GIVE RICHLY! If you want to be poor...GRASP and be GREEDY! If you want abundance...SCATTER GOOD SEED ABUNDANTLY! If you want to be NEEDY...HOARD and HIDE the good seed! With this in mind, let's explore God's Seven Irrefutable Laws of the Harvest.

Law One—We Reap Only What We Sow

For centuries it was widely believed that some things just automatically came into existence out of nowhere and from nothing. The scientist Louis Pasteur revealed the fallacy of this belief when he convincingly demonstrated that there is no such thing as spontaneous generation. Nothing comes into existence in and of itself. Every effect has a corresponding cause. This is a law of nature that has been written by the Creator of the universe. All life comes from antecedent life: from the labor and sowing of others. What we reap was planted either naturally or purposely, either by God or by man, and for either positive or for negative results. We reap the fruit of much for which we have extended no labor, because we enter into the labor of others either for good or for bad.

In spite of Pasteur's findings, many persons still live with an I-can-get-something-for-nothing attitude that violates the basic, built in laws of the harvest. However, one might just as well believe that they can break the laws of gravity and jump from the Empire State building expecting an enjoyable trip down and a safe landing upon arrival at the street, as to think that they can reap if they never sow. God has Spiritual Laws as well as natural laws that are immutable (do not change), inviolable (cannot be violated), and universal (apply equally to everyone).

A seed has great potential for a future harvest, but irrespective of its fertile DNA, until it is sown in the proper soil at the proper time, it is barren and unfruitful. If a farmer plants no seed, he can believe God for a miracle but it will be highly unlikely that God would grant it. If He did, it would be a rare exception and not the general rule. On the other hand, if the farmer plants good seed in good soil at the right time, it would also require either a catastrophe like a flood or fire, or a miracle for him not to reap a harvest, because whatsoever a man sows that shall he also reap.

The writer of the book of Ecclesiastes sets forth the inexcusability of not facing up

There is no excuse for not sowing.

to our responsibility in observing the laws of sowing and reaping: *"Whoever watches the wind will not plant; whoever looks at the clouds will not reap."*[2] This says in essence that there is no excuse for not sowing irrespective of how unpropitious our situations may appear. This applies not only to farming but to all of life. There is nothing more exhausting and impoverishing in life than constantly searching for an easy way to make a living. The easy way up is usually the quickest way down. Sowing involves time and tenacity, not the latest instant promises to bypass the efforts of the laws of the harvest. Remember, there is no reaping without sowing.

Law Two — We Reap What We Sow

This basic law of nature is an integral part of God's creation. The principle was repeated over and over in the creation account. *"Then God said, 'Let the land produce vegetation: seed-bearing plants and trees on the land that bear fruit with seed in it, according to their various kinds.' And so it was so. The land produced vegetation: plants bearing seed according to their kinds and trees bearing fruit with seed in it according to their kinds. And God saw that it was good."*[3]

Every seed carries its own unique DNA. If we plant good seed, we can expect good fruit. If we plant a bad seed, we can

> *Every seed carries its own unique DNA.*

expect bad fruit. As simplistic as it seems in the natural realm, knowing that if we want corn we cannot get it by sowing wheat, yet in all other realms of life we somehow feel that we can sow anger, bitterness, unforgiveness, unfriendliness, selfishness and reap love, joy, peace, friendships and edifying relationships. DUH!

People are constantly coming to me with confessions of disappointment in their harvest. They say, Brother Paul, "Nobody loves me." I respond with a law-of-the-harvest question, "Who are you sowing your love into? How and what type of love are you giving away?" Is it an eros type love with the self-referential hook on it that is always trying to draw people into your life to meet your needs? Or is it the agape type of love that gives to meet the needs of others without expecting anything in return?

If you want encouragement then you must sow the seed of

being an encourager. If you are always coming up short in the realm of blessings, you should stop and ask what kind of blessings you have sown into the lives of other people and ministries.

One cannot sow hatred, bitterness, and unforgiveness and expect life. The DNA of these seeds can only produce death. However, if you sow love, peace and forgiveness, these seeds will eventually produce life in abundance because that is their genetic type.

> *Instead of regulating, we need to resolve issues.*

Far too many people spend the majority of their adult lives trying to regulate the fruit or the harvest of the sowing of bad seeds instead of resolving the issues by going to the root of the problem and changing the seed and sowing habits of their daily lives. The majority of today's counseling is an attempt to enable people to learn to regulate or cope with the bad fruit in their lives. Instead they should be confronted with truth in love for the purpose of dealing with the root issues that cause the fruit issuances. They need to be told that it is only by radically and consistently changing the type of seed they have been sowing that they will change the harvest they are getting. Instead of regulating, we need to resolve issues at the root and the root has everything to do with seed.

We need to examine our sowing and harvest practices.

We must always sow with a specific plan in mind. There are many things about life that require us to deal with that which someone else has sown or with things that we have no control over, such as automobile accidents, wars, epidemics, loss of job, loved ones, etc. Yet there are still many areas in which we get to choose the seed that we plant and the nature and amount of our harvest.

There is an old Chinese proverb that says the journey of a thousand miles begins with the first step.

Plan to make positive and potentially productive steps, not negative and most certainly destructive ones.

The first step toward a better and bigger harvest is not a misstep that you made in the past, but your next step made today. Plan to make it positive and potentially productive, not negative and most certainly destructive. Make it a step that is forward-focused and not past-obsessed. Aim well at the designated target and don't randomly shoot at anything that moves. Sow in such a manner that your life is lived by design and not by default. The steps you take today become the well worn path of tomorrow's success, not a rut that resembles a grave!

Sow the best of seeds in the best prepared places for top-quality harvests. Mark Twain said, "When you need a friend, it's too late to make one." It is always the choice of the farmer to select which crops to cultivate. The laws of the harvest are inviolable and apply universally. *"A man reaps what he sows."* [4] Proverbs reminds us that if we want friends, we must show (sow) ourselves friendly.

Take pride in your sowing and in the fruit, but don't take all the credit. We reap much because of the previous labors of others and the present help of partners, friends and other businesses. Maintain an attitude of gratitude for your team and be sure to share the harvest with all your co-laborers. Today we are enjoying in World Wide Dream Builders the fruit of the seed sown decades ago. That encourages me to sow for future generations spiritually, relationally and materially.

Law Three — We Reap in a Different Season than We Sow

When a farmer goes out and plants his seed in the ground, he does not plan on coming out the very next day with his combine to start reaping the harvest. He knows that there must first be a long period of growth. Several months will pass before the season of harvest will arrive. During this time of waiting, there is always the temptation to believe that the harvest will not come to pass.

It has been my ongoing experience that good things sown into people's lives thirty years ago, that seemed to have rotted in the soil of ingratitude and forgetfulness, surprise me with a generous harvest from time to time. There's a generous gift from a pastor we ministered to twenty-five years ago; there's an invitation for us to take a free vacation in someone's condo that we ministered to and gave time and invested monies some five years ago. We thought they had forgotten to even say thank you.

> *Overnight success is a two to five year plan!*

Someone put it well when they said, "Overnight success is a two to five year plan!" Instant success is an oxymoron—it just doesn't exist.

Patience is needed to persist in your sowing and cultivation until the harvest is ready, not just when you are ready to start reaping. Remember, John Mason describes impatience as "one big get-a-headache!"

This contemporary generation of Americans has grown up in an "instant" age. We have instant coffee, instant tea, instant potatoes, instant winners, and instant pain relief. We have become so accustomed to receiving everything "instantly" that we have great difficulty waiting for anything.

One newly arrived immigrant to America was taken by his sponsor into a large grocery where he saw sights like never before. They passed by one shelf and the boxes read "Instant Potatoes." Not understanding, the immigrant asked what it meant. The sponsor informed him that all that was required was to pour out the powder and add water and heat and you would have instant mashed potatoes. They came to the "Instant Coffee" and the immigrant said, "Let me guess— pour the powder out, add water and heat and you have coffee ready to drink." Thinking his new friend understood, they walked on through the store until they came to a shelf that had boxes of "Baby Powder." To which the man cried, "Boy, America is something else! Open the box, pour out the powder and add water and heat and you have a new baby!" His little understanding had led him to a total misunderstanding! This is the typical attitude of so many Americans today. Get it off of a store shelf, open it up and follow a few simple, short instructions, and you have instant food, instant drink, instant fun, instant financial success, instant love, etc!

As Americans, we aren't short on too many things. Praise God for His

There is a severe shortage in most of our lives... a shortage of patience!

mercy in making ours a land of abundance. However, there is a severe shortage in most of our lives—a shortage of patience. We all know that we need and even want patience—but we want it right now! We aren't into waiting on anything. Again, we are into "working" for the Lord, but not into "waiting" on the Lord.

Before James A. Garfield was President of the USA, he was principal of Hiram College in Ohio. A father once asked him if a particular course of study couldn't be simplified so that his son could go through by a shorter route.

"Certainly," replied Garfield. "But it all depends upon what you want to make of your boy. When God wants to make an oak tree, he takes a hundred years. When he wants to make a squash, he requires only one summer."

> *We are into "working" for the Lord, not into "waiting" on the Lord.*

God is intent upon making boys into godly men who are like trees of righteousness for generations to come. Thus, He is very patient and knows that our impatience would circumvent His design and make us fat squashes instead of giant oaks for God. So for this reason, He won't let the development of patience be an optional extra—for some and not for others.

God's Tests that Measure Our Patience Level

1. Interruptions—How do you deal with interruptions in your schedule? These are unscheduled visits, events or circumstances that happen. You know what I mean: when you sit down for dinner and the phone rings, or somebody comes to the door, or you are on your way to somewhere and you find you have a flat tire and you stop to fix it and find that your spare tire is flat also! Now, I'm not tooting my own horn when I share this. You will remember the Lord said, "He that tooteth his own horn weareth down his own battery." However, I am learning in life the joy of interruptions, because the older I get the more I realize that God has allowed them to happen for some divine reason, which is far greater than my understanding. Ultimately, when I respond to God instead of reacting to the situation and my eyes are opened, I can always see someone to whom God wants me to minister.

2. Inconveniences—When we are asked to do things that are not convenient, that don't fit so nicely in our schedule, how do we respond? How do you deal with delays, tardy people, and bothersome intrusions? How do you deal with the inconveniences of life?

3. Irritations—How do you deal with those little things in life that just seem to rub you the wrong way? Things like: traffic jams, long lines, phone calls, misplaced keys, no service at the restaurant, late people, late buses or planes, obnoxious people, car trouble, bad manners, broken machines, no shows, etc.

4. Inactivity—Most of us would rather do anything than wait. We hate to have to wait for a parking space. We hate to wait in line at the grocery store, the dentist office, and the doctor's office. We hate to wait in traffic. Someone, somehow, has figured out that city dwellers will spend approximately 6 months of their life sitting at red lights waiting for them to turn green. How you deal with inactivity demonstrates whether or not there is true genuine patience in your life.

There was a truck driver who stopped one night at an all night restaurant in Broken Bow, Nebraska. The waitress had just brought out his meal when three bikers came into the restaurant. For some reason they singled him out to apparently pick a fight. One grabbed his hamburger, another took a handful of fries and the third took his coffee and began to drink it. Instead of getting mad and going at them, the trucker picked up his check, left a tip,

> *Who can tell just when the seed is germinating?*

paid for his meal and walked out. The waitress watched him leave and went to serve the bikers. One of the bikers looked at her and said, "Not much of a man is he?" The waitress said, "Not much of a truck driver either, he just ran over three motorcycles in the parking lot." The man didn't really pass the patience test.

If God's process of bringing our lives and labor to harvest is like those of farming, we will often be working in the dark places at different paces! So much of farming is hidden beneath the soil or behind the leaves. Anyone can see the cornfield, but who can tell just when the seed is germinating? Yet, even greater is the mystery of when and how, before the seed ever gives signs of germination, it receives its first thrill of awaking and resurrection life. How much goes on in the dark!

Great harvests may have begun at the very time that we are trudging home with laboring feet and weeping eyes, bemoaning our long and fruitless and inefficient day. This picture of the farmer is relatable to you and me, as indeed it must have been to these tired and discouraged workers in the early church. *"Let us not become weary in doing good, for at the proper time we will reap a harvest if we do not give up."* [5] Don't start to rest on your rake! Without a regular maintenance program, your field will turn into a jungle.

"But the seed on good soil stands for those with a noble and good heart, who hear the word, retain it, and by persevering produce a crop." [6]

"We do not want you to become lazy, but to imitate those who through faith and patience inherit what has been promised." [7]

"Be patient, then, brothers, until the Lord's coming. See how the farmer waits for the land to yield its valuable crop and how patient he is for the autumn and spring rains." [8]

Patient persons aren't those who never fail, but those who never quit. Changing from the farming metaphor to that of baseball, we need reminding that stopping at third base adds no more score than striking out. The measure of true success is not just getting a big hit, but making it safely home.

An early church father, Tertullian, realized the imperativeness of patience in the children of God and wrote, "Patience commends us to God, and keeps us His. Patience is the guardian of faith, the preserver of peace, the cherisher of love, the teacher of humility. Patience governs the flesh, strengthens the spirit, sweetens the temper, stifles anger, extinguishes envy, subdues pride, bridles the tongue, refrains the hand, tramples upon temptations, endures persecutions, and consummates martyrdom. Patience produces unity in the church, loyalty in the state, harmony in soci-

> *Patience produces unity, loyalty, harmony & peace.*

ety, and peace in families. She comforts the poor, and moderates the rich. She makes us meek in prosperity, cheerful in adversity, and unmoved by reproach. She teaches us to for-

give those who injure us, and to be the first in asking forgiveness of those we have injured. She adorns the woman,
and approves the man; is loved in the child, praised in the
youth, and admired in the old. She rides not in the whirlwind and the stormy tempest of passion, but her throne is the
humble and contrite heart, and her kingdom the kingdom of
peace."

Law Four—We Reap Significantly and Proportionately More Than We Sow

There would be no farmers if this principle were not true.
When a farmer sacrifices several bushels of corn by planting
them in the ground, he does so with the expectations that his
efforts will be rewarded with hundreds of bushels in the coming harvest.

However, every farmer understands that you establish the
size of your harvest when you sow the seed. If you want a
large harvest then you must sow generously. Yet, when it
comes to relationships, finances and the productivity of one's
business, or one's spiritual growth, there is a tendency to
somehow think that we can violate this law and give a little
while expecting a lot. We expect to put forth a little effort and
reap a great business;. We believe we can invest a few minutes
a day in the lives of our children and reap a vibrant and
loving relationship with them. We think we can read
scripture and pray five minutes once a month and grow into
spiritual maturity.

The scriptures set forth the fourth law of the harvest very

clearly: *"Remember this: Whoever sows sparingly will also reap sparingly, and whoever sows generously will also reap generously."* [9]

Everyone who got where he is had to begin where he was using what he had! An abundant harvest will not be the lot of the person who sits around wishing and waiting to sow because of what he does not have or because he does not have the amount that some of his peers have.

As the waitress watched, Andy said, "Ma'am, we're going to need more sugar for this table." This Texas waitress looked at Andy and said, "Listen, bud, before I give you more sugar, you stir what you got." There is a great truth in this statement—Stir what you got—Use your gifts. Start sowing the seed that you have instead of waiting and wishing for more seed or a different type seed, or a better situation in which to sow.

Just like any of the other seven laws, this law also works in the negative. We are told in Hosea, *"They sow the wind and reap the whirlwind."* [10] Those that sow to the flesh shall reap destruction.

In the book of Genesis there is a great illustration of the above verse in the life of the old patriarch Jacob. As a result of sowing the wind, Jacob (whose name means supplanter or deceiver) reaped the whirlwind of trouble and heartache. His mother Rebecca schemed with her second born son Jacob to deceive his father to steal the family blessing. Because of this, Jacob was forced to flee because his brother Esau had sworn that after his father's death he would kill Jacob. Rebecca sent Jacob away for what she thought would be only a few days. But she never saw Jacob again because he was gone for twenty years.

Jacob had schemed and deceived to get the blessing, and later he would receive in kind and even more from Laban, his future father-in-law.   Jacob worked seven years to marry Rachel and was tricked by Laban into marrying Leah, the oldest daughter. Jacob then worked another seven years for Rachel.

Jacob used the skin of a kid goat to deceive his father Isaac. In his old age he was deceived by his sons into believing that his son was dead, when they showed him the goat skin coat Joseph had worn covered with blood. *""He who sows wickedness reaps trouble, and the rod of his fury will be destroyed." 11*

Law Five — We Reap the Full Harvest Only if We Persevere

Perhaps no passage of scripture sets forth this truth as succinctly and auspiciously as *"Let us not become weary in doing good, for at the proper time we will reap a harvest if we do not give up. " 12*

> *You must seed for success or you'll be weeding for failure.*

Someone stated law five a little more illuminatingly when they declared: "We reap the full harvest of the good only if we persevere; the evil comes to harvest on its own." A farmer or gardener knows that he has to plant seeds for the harvest, but he doesn't have to plant weeds. They come about on their own. "...the evil comes to harvest on its own."

Irrespective of how promising the growing crop looks, if

we stop nurturing it generously, weeding it carefully, watering it regularly, fertilizing it as needed, guarding it against encroaching animals and insects, then we will get little fruit and a field of weeds. Only weeds flourish in an environment of indifference. This applies across the board as well—husband and wife relationships, friendships, parent/child relationships, business, relationships upline and downline, athletics, and spiritual matters as well—all require patience, constant and careful attention, and persistence until the very end. Failure usually comes when we take the path of least resistance while living on the route of least persistence. Neglect is the subtle killer of our generation. The writer of Hebrews said, *"How shall we escape if we neglect so great a salvation."* [13] A marriage neglected, a business neglected, a relationship neglected, our finances neglected, health neglected, our salvation neglected, can end in great devastation. What do you have to do to destroy your life in every area? Absolutely nothing!!

The Apostle Paul says that we need to persevere in doing good. We need to keep on doing good, even when we are not noticed, even when we don't feel like it, and even when we are discouraged. The writer of the book of Hebrews, addressing a group of believers who

> *To know and not do is not yet to know.*

were on the verge of giving up due to the extremely difficult circumstances that they were going through reminded them that it is always too soon to quit: *"For you have need of patience, that, after you have done the will of God, you might receive the promise. For yet a little while, and he that shall come will come, and will not tarry."* [14]

What You Seed is What You Get!

One man said, "To know and not do is not yet to know." Probably all of us at one time or another could readily say concerning the hard persevering work prior to the harvest, "I know that!" Those who have gardens know that you cannot plant and forget. The problem of the average American today is not a lack of knowledge, but the application of truths he already knows.

There are three essentials in regards to persevering until the harvest.

1. There must be correct planting. Remember, some seeds have a short shelf life and they must be sown before the expiration date. With this type of seed, we must have a sense of urgency. The good seeds that are in your possession can save a marriage in trouble, a business that is being mismanaged, a life that is being destroyed by wrong choices, if you take advantage of the opportune moment and plant them now. You cannot do the right thing too soon.

2. There must be consistent cultivation. You are faced with choices everyday that require the consistent cultivation of faith or doubt, trust or distrust, hope or despair, positive expectations or negative. Whatever you feed is what will grow. If you feed faith, it will grow. If you feed worry and fear, they will grow up to choke out the root of faith and trust. Fertilizing is a messy job, but always worth the effort.

Fertilizing is a messy job, but always worth the effort.

All of us have our moments of doubt. When this is your experience, then keep doubt private, but make faith public.

3. There must be constant attention. We must give constant attention to those factors that would choke, nibble to shreds, and displace the main plants in the fields of our lives. We cannot make wrong, evil or sinful choices work in the end. Yes, it may appear to be working, but payday has not fully come. Someone said it well when they remarked that "life is always an uphill battle for those who are not on the level!"

Truth, in the end, will always win out over the lie; love will win out over hatred, forgiveness will win out over bitterness and unforgiveness. Despite the fact that in our present day truth seems to be forever on the scaffold and wrong on the throne, but dear friend, God's truth will always ultimately triumph.

Without constant attention to our field, we will get so busy doing things other than the main things that we will lose the harvest. In the organization that I pastor, one of the leaders made an insightful and significant statement when they said, "Most people don't really quit the business, they just get so busy with other things that the business just doesn't fit in any more." Remember that I referred to petty interests earlier. Anything other than your ultimate purpose is a petty interest in your life.

Keep doubt private, but make faith public.

There are two things that are guaranteed to bring crop failure and devastation into your life: One, take everybody's counsel; two, take nobody's counsel.

What You Seed is What You Get!

Law Six—It is too Late to do Anything about Last Year's Harvest, but it's Never too Soon to begin Sowing for a Future Harvest!

> *Remember a lie will add to your troubles, subtract from your energy, multiply your difficulties, and divide your effectiveness.*

Life can be understood backwards, but it must be lived forwards. If you had to choose between memory and sight, which would you choose? For me, I would choose sight, because it is far better to see where you are going than to remember where you have been.

In 1954, Opening Day of Baseball, the Cincinnati Reds played the Milwaukee Braves. Two rookies started in that game. Cincinnati had a rookie named Jim Greengrass who went 4 for 4 with four doubles—WOW! The other rookie went 0 for 4, but that was just his first day. After their retirement, Jim Greengrass went on to start his own lawn care company and most of us have never heard of him again.

Who was the other rookie who went 0 for 4? His name was Hank Aaron. He went on to become the greatest home run hitter in major league baseball history.

You may have a life that is strewn with mistakes and blunders, you may have struck out and seem to have gone 0 for 4 in last year's harvest, but the question is, "Which direction are you heading? How do you want to finish?" Yesterday has gone into the tomb of time and tomorrow is still in the womb of time, but today is the opportune time to begin to sow the type of seeds that will produce a future harvest.

Remember, some people grin and bear it, while others smile and change it. Hard times can be turned into harvest times when you stop whining when crops fail and begin nurturing what is left or replanting for the future harvest that you have envisioned.

Crop-failures happen to the best of farmers. This is true in every other area of life as well. The difference between failure and success often lies in how one handles crop failures.

There are three basic responses to crop-failures that we mentioned earlier but would like to explore further now:

1. Cover Up—You can blame other for the consequences of your choices. President Bush was asked in an interview by Larry King how it was that he could make decisions so quickly and then stick by them. He responded by saying that it was easy, because he had some core values that were non-negotiable and every decision was run through those values. Then he rested on them and stood by

> Remember some people grin and bear it, while others smile and change it.

them. If you have the right core values when a decision is made and it is obviously wrong, those values won't allow you to lie, shift the blame or cover up. Instead you accept the responsibility, admit that you were wrong, seek proper counsel and move forward. To cover up is to bury bad seed that will spring up producing bad fruit.

2. Give Up—Once, when going through some very difficult times due to bad seed sown on my part, some of my friends counseled me to just give up and go back to the old life and ways. My response was, "Go back to what? Go back to where? Is that a joke? There is nothing to go back to!" During a time when things weren't going as planned, the Lord asked Peter a question. "Will

> *Life can be understood backwards but it must be lived forwards.*

you too go away?" Others had already turned back. Peter's response should be the core response of our commitment in life. Our commitment to the Lord must be 'for better or worse." He is our source, our force and our course. Peter said, "Lord, where am I going to go? You alone have the words of eternal life. You alone care about me." God has shown us a better way, friend, and because of that we should never even entertain going back, because there is nothing there!

> *Talk encouragement instead of discouragement.*

We must delete from our vocabulary statements that are like bad seeds: "I can't!" "If only..." "I'm a failure!" "The best days are behind me!" and other similar statements. Begin to practice being an affirmer of people and not a complainer about and to people. Talk encouragement instead of discouragement; build people up instead of blasting them to bits; bless them instead of cursing them. Confess faith in God and the faith of God for victory, instead of fear of loss and defeat.

The mouth is the biggest seed planter we possess and the words it sows are the biggest crop producers. When you open your mouth to speak, what comes out reveals that your heart is either full of grace, or fouled by sin; that your head is full of wisdom, or empty. When you open your mouth, you pull back the curtain of your heart and let people see what is inside. Yes, you may deceive some of the people some of the time, but you will not deceive the spiritually discerning. They will know that what you are saying is inconsistent with your lifestyle. Someone has said that if your mind should go blank, don't forget to turn off the sound by shutting your mouth!

Our mind should be the mind of Christ. Our words should be words touched by the Holy Spirit. And our deeds should be consistent with His. "What would Jesus do," is more than an in vogue wristband; it's a way of life. Jesus does more than think or speak, He acts. Consider this humorous, but revealing story.

A man fell into a pit and could not get himself out.

A subjective person came along and said, "I feel for you down there."

An objective person came along and said, "Well, it's logical that someone would fall in that pit."

A Christian scientist came along and said, "You only think that you're in that pit."

A Pharisee said, "Only bad people fall in pits."

A Mathematician calculated how he fell into the pit.

A Fundamentalist said, "You deserve your pit."

A Pentecostal said, "If you'd been saved, you'd never fallen in that pit."

A Baptist said, "You were saved and still fell in that pit."

A Charismatic said, "Just confess that you're not in that pit."

A Calvinist said, "Before the foundations of the world, that pit was dug for you."

A News Reporter wanted an exclusive on how he fell in his pit.

A Realist said, "Now, that's a pit."

A Geologist told him to appreciate the rock strata in the pit.

An IRS agent asked if he was paying taxes on the pit.

The County Inspector asked if he had a permit to dig the pit.

The evasive person came by and avoided the subject all together.

A self-pitying person said, "You haven't seen anything until you've seen my pit."

An optimist said, "Things could be worse."

A pessimist said, "Things will get worse."

Jesus, seeing the man, reached down and took him by the hand and lifted him out of the pit.

3. **Stand Up**—This is the only logical, right, biblical and crop-failure-fixing response. It means that we stop trying to run away from the consequences of our poor choices, assume responsibility, and begin to change the seed we are sowing in anticipation that, although it is too late to do anything about last year's harvest, it's never too soon to begin sowing for a future harvest.

Law Seven—The Harvest Must be Reaped and Properly Handled if the Seed is to be Reproduced!

In the makeup of the seed, we learn that God has designed it so that it not only reproduces itself, but transfers and transmits its life and treasure to the next generation. To insure that there is reproduction and generational transfer of our life and treasure, we must not fail at the strategic time of reaping and handling of the ripe harvest.

Let me make four suggestions as to the proper method of handling the seed of your harvest:

1. Make sure that a portion of your harvest is given to God.

2. Make sure that a portion of your harvest is enjoyed by yourself.

3. Make sure that you save a portion of your harvest for the future.

4. Make sure that a portion of your harvest is sown back into your fields.

There was an Indian chief that had a reputation throughout the Indian nations as being the most successful rain dancer that ever existed. His record was impeccable. Every time he danced, it rained. Due to the lack of success on the part of so many other rain-dancers, they decided to have a conference on "The Art of Successful Rain-dancing." They assembled all the rain dancers from throughout the Indian nations. Each was given an opportunity to talk about their philosophy, practices, and procedures in rain dancing. They realized that they all had one thing in common, they had failed many times in attempting to make it rain.

The renowned, always successful rain dancer had kept silent throughout the conference. Finally, they all got quiet in the presence of the old chief and one of them asked him what was the secret of his phenomenal success was in making it rain every time he danced. The old chief said, "Uhh, I just keep on dancing until it rains!"

So stop wishing and start working; stop proposing and start purposing; stop talking and start dancing! The harvest you are longing for is coming, if you keep on keeping on until it comes to fruition!

The poem of the turnip seeds sums up all that we have been saying: **If Turnip Seeds Grow Turnips**

If turnip seeds grow turnips,
 And greens grown spinach greens;
If carrot seeds grow carrots,
 And bean seeds bring up beans;
If lettuce seeds grow lettuce,
 And brussel seeds grow sprouts;
If pea seeds always bring up peas—
 Then what goes in comes out!

So kind words bring up kindness,
 And bad words will grow sadness;
Forgiving words will grow forgiveness,
 Glad words will grow gladness!
So watch the little seeds you plant,
 In all you say and do;
For what you sow is what you reap!
 Be proud of what you grew!

Let's all end well by God's grace and be proud of what we grew in life.

Just remember, What You Seed is What You Get!

Appendix

CHAPTER 1

[1] 2 Corinthians 9:10

[2] I Peter 1:23

[3] Matthew 13:3-8

[4] Matthew 13:23

[5] Genesis 1:11-12

[6] Genesis 1:29-31

[7] Genesis 8:22

[8] John 12:24

[9] Mark 4:30-32

[10] Matthew 13:33

[11] Isaiah 49:6

[12] Ecclesiastes 11:1-6

[13] John 4:38

[14] Matthew 25:23

[15] Mark 4:26-29

[16] John 12:24-25

[17] 2 Corinthians 9:6

[18] Matthew 13:24-30

[19] Galatians 6:9

What You Seed is What You Get!

CHAPTER 2

1 Ecclesiastes 11:1
2 Ecclesiastes 11:2
3 Luke 6:38
4 2 Corinthians 9:6
5 Ecclesiastes 11:4-6
6 Ecclesiastes 11:3-4
7 Psalm 118:24
8 Ecclesiastes 11:3b
9 Psalm 118:24
10 Ecclesiastes 11:5
11 Ecclesiastes 11:6

CHAPTER 3

1 Proverbs 18:21
2 James 3:2
3 Proverbs 6:2
4 Proverbs 12:13-14
5 Proverbs 12:18
6 Proverbs 12:19
7 Proverbs 15:4
8 Proverbs 18:21
9 Proverbs 21:23
10 James 3:9-12
11 Numbers 22:6
12 James 3:11-12
13 1 Samuel 15:23
14 James 3:18
15 Galatians 3:8-9
16 Galatians 3:14
17 Acts 3:26
18 Romans 12:14

[19] James 3:15-17

[20] Psalm 34:1

[21] Genesis 49:25

CHAPTER 4

[1] Galatians 6:9

[2] James 5:7

[3] James 1:3

[4] Mark 4:26-29

[5] Isaiah 30:18

[6] James 5:8

[7] Psalm 62:1-2

[8] Psalm 33:20

[9] Psalm 27:14

[10] James 5:9

[11] Philippians 2:14

[12] 1 Corinthians 10:10

[13] Numbers 14:2-4

[14] Isaiah 40:21

[15] James 3:17

[16] Luke 8:15

[17] Hebrews 6:12

[18] Hebrews 10:36-37

[19] James 5:7

[20] Galatians 6:9

CHAPTER 5

[1] Matthew 7:1-2

[2] Genesis 18:20-21

[3] Romans 14:1

[4] Acts 20:35b

[5] Matthew 23:23

6   Psalm 126:5-6

7   John 3:16

8   Romans 8:32

CHAPTER 6

1   Luke 12:15-21

2   Luke 12:15b

3   Proverbs 1:32

4   Luke 12:19

5   Luke 12:20

6   Luke 12:17-19

7   Proverbs 30:8-9

8   Luke 12:20-21

9   Luke 10:30-35

10   Malachi 3:10a

11   Malachi 3:8

12   Luke 21:3-4

13   2 Corinthians 8:5

14   2 Timothy 2:6

15   Proverbs 22:7

16   Proverbs 6:6-8

CHAPTER 7

1   James 1:2-4

2   Ephesians 3:10

3   Mark 4:26-29

4   Philippians 3:8

5   Luke 16:10-12

6   Proverbs 24:17

7   Psalm 37:23-24

CHAPTER 8

[1] Hosea 8:7

[2] Ecclesiastes 11:4

[3] Genesis 1:11-12

[4] Galatians 6:7b

[5] Galatians 6:9

[6] Luke 8:15

[7] Hebrews 6:12

[8] James 5:7

[9] 2 Corinthians 9:6

[10] Hosea 8:7

[11] Proverbs 22:8

[12] Galatians 6:9

[13] Hebrews 2:3

[14] Hebrews 10:36

For additional resources from Paul E. Tsika Ministries Inc.
write:

Restoration Ranch
P. O. Box 136
Midfield, TX 77458

or see our website:
www.plowon.org
Office Phone: 361-588-7190

NOTES

NOTES

NOTES

NOTES

NOTES

NOTES